Also by Bob Woodward

PLAN OF ATTACK

BUSH AT WAR

MAESTRO: GREENSPAN'S FED AND THE AMERICAN BOOM

SHADOW: FIVE PRESIDENTS AND THE LEGACY OF WATERGATE

THE CHOICE

THE AGENDA: INSIDE THE CLINTON WHITE HOUSE

THE COMMANDERS

VEIL: THE SECRET WARS OF THE CIA 1981–1987

WIRED: THE SHORT LIFE AND FAST TIMES OF JOHN BELUSHI

THE BRETHREN (with Scott Armstrong)

THE FINAL DAYS (with Carl Bernstein)

ALL THE PRESIDENT'S MEN (with Carl Bernstein)

THE SECRET MAN

THE STORY OF WATERGATE'S
DEEP THROAT

BOB WOODWARD

SIMON & SCHUSTER

NEW YORK LONDON TORONTO SYDNEY

Simon & Schuster
Rockefeller Center
1230 Avenue of the Americas
New York, NY 10020

For information regarding special discounts for bulk purchases,
please contact Simon & Schuster Special Sales at 1-800-456-6798
or business@simonandschuster.com

Designed by C. Linda Dingler

Manufactured in the United States of America

1   3   5   7   9   10   8   6   4   2

ISBN-13: 978-0-7432-8715-9
ISBN-10: 0-7432-8715-0

To
*Katharine Graham, Ben Bradlee,
and Alice Mayhew*

1

IN FEBRUARY 1992, AS THE 20TH ANNIVERSARY OF the Watergate break-in approached, I went to the fortress-like J. Edgar Hoover FBI headquarters building on Pennsylvania Avenue in Washington. An imposing cement structure with large dark windows, the Hoover building sits appropriately about midway between the White House and the Capitol. It is as if Hoover, the founding director and the embodiment of the FBI from 1924 to 1972, is still present in Washington, D.C., playing off presidents against the Congress. I navigated the labyrinth of security and finally made my way to the documents room. I had come to examine some of the FBI's investigative Watergate files that had been opened to the public. Private cubicles are available in the classy, law-firm atmosphere, well lit, all done in high-quality wood paneling well above the standard government issue. The room is quiet. I was offered blue-lined paper to take notes.

The Watergate files contain hundreds of internal FBI memos, requests for action, investigative summaries, and Teletypes to headquarters from field offices which had conducted hundreds of interviews. There were the first summaries of information on the five burglars arrested in the Democrats' Watergate office building headquarters: their names, their backgrounds, their CIA connections, and their contacts with E. Howard Hunt Jr., the former CIA operative and White House consultant, and G. Gordon Liddy, the former FBI agent. The files teemed with notes, routing slips and queries bearing initials from senior Bureau officials, dates and intelligence classifications.

The outline of the Watergate cover-up was so clear in retrospect. White House counsel John W. Dean III, who later confessed to leading the illegal obstruction of justice on behalf of President Richard Nixon, "stated all requests for investigation by FBI at White House must be cleared through him," according to a summary dated six days after the June 17, 1972, break-in.

A memo on October 10, 1972, addressed *The Washington Post* story that Carl Bernstein and I had written that day. It was probably our most important story; it reported that the Watergate break-in was not an isolated event but "stemmed from a massive campaign of political spying and sabotage" run by the White House and President Nixon's reelection committee. The two-page memo stated that the FBI had learned that Donald H. Segretti, who headed the efforts to harass Democratic presidential candidates, had been hired by Dwight L. Chapin, the president's appointments secretary, and paid by Herbert W. Kalmbach, the president's personal lawyer. Because there was no direct connection to the Watergate bugging, the memo said, the FBI had not pursued the matter.

I smiled. Here were two of the reasons the Watergate cover-up had worked at first: Dean's effectiveness in squelching further inquiry; and the seeming utter lack of imagination on the part of the FBI.

All of this was a pleasant, long, well-documented reminder of names, events and emotions as I sifted through the Bureau memos, as best I could tell almost a complete set of internal memos and investigative files. The files and memos provided a kind of intimacy with what had been four intense years of my life, as Carl Bernstein and I covered the story for *The Washington Post* and wrote two books about Watergate: *All the President's Men*, published in 1974, which was about our newspaper's investigation; and *The Final Days*, published in 1976, which chronicled the collapse of the Nixon presidency.

At the time of my visit I was 48 years old, but I was not

there for a trip down memory lane. I was not hunting for more information in the rich history of Watergate; not looking for new avenues, leads, surprises, contradictions, unrevealed crimes or hidden meaning, although the amazements of Watergate rarely ceased.

Instead, I was really there in further pursuit of Deep Throat—the celebrated, secret anonymous source who had helped direct our Watergate coverage during late-night meetings in an underground parking garage. The *Post's* managing editor, Howard Simons, had dubbed the source Deep Throat, after the pornographic movie of the time, because the interviews were technically on "deep background"—a journalistic term meaning that the information can be used but no source of any kind would be identified in the newspaper.

Only six people knew Deep Throat's identity besides Deep Throat himself: me, Carl, my wife Elsa Walsh, former *Post* executive editor Benjamin C. Bradlee and later his successor, Leonard Downie Jr., and a Justice Department lawyer who discovered the secret in 1976. More on that later.

Despite all the guesses and speculation, articles and books, no one else had pinned down his identity. The more names and lists that had been floated over the decades, the more clouded the trail seemed to become. Systematic, meticulous analysis, even books by Nixon Watergate lawyers John Dean and Leonard Garment, had failed to illuminate because Deep Throat himself had embedded part of his identity in *not* being such a source, not the man in the underground garage so memorably portrayed by actor Hal Holbrook in the movie *All the President's Men*. Wise, almost Delphic, but convoluted, creepy and angry, Holbrook had captured the real Deep Throat's side of one of the most clandestine relationships in American journalism. In our conversations at the time, the real Deep Throat had clearly been torn, and even uncertain—not fully convinced that helping us was the proper course, wanting both to do it and not do it. Like many if not most confidential sources he wanted to be free of the ramifications of his actions and words. He wanted to be protected at nearly any cost, and he had gone to extraordinary lengths to conceal his identity. As best I could tell he had lied to his colleagues, friends and even his family. He had been in hiding and still was.

I was there at the Hoover building that day in 1992 because Deep Throat had worked in the very center of the FBI. His position gave him access to information from hundreds, eventually thousands of interviews and documents in the first months after the 1972 burglary. In addition, he was well situated to learn much about the Nixon White House, its behavior and concealment strategies. Facts, leads and even rumors about Nixon, Washington and politics came to his desk and ears. He could draw on the raw data in FBI files. He was able to provide all kinds of clues, ultimately giving us the schematic diagram of the Watergate conspiracy, or at least pointing us to it.

In *All the President's Men,* Carl and I identified Deep Throat as someone in the executive branch of the government whose position was "extremely sensitive." Many took this, incorrectly, to mean it was someone in the Nixon White House.

In an attempt to determine who was behind the break-in, Carl and I had spent months going down through a list of people who had worked at the Committee for the Re-election of the President (CREEP was its unfortunate acronym), tracking them down by phone or in person at their homes in D.C. or the Washington suburbs. Carl was driven and systematic, haunting people. One person he talked to was CREEP's bookkeeper, later identified as Judy Hoback. During several interviews at her home she described for us in detail how Liddy and other close assistants to John N. Mitchell, the former attorney general and then head of CREEP, had been given hundreds of thousands of dollars in cash for campaign espionage and dirty tricks. As I went through the FBI files, I found the "302" form of Hoback's interview with the FBI. She had described to them exactly what she told Carl and me. We had written it in the *Post,* leading many FBI agents to conclude, incorrectly, that we were getting raw FBI reports.

Deep Throat never provided exact details from these

302 reports. He confirmed the breadth of questionable and illegal activities by CREEP and the White House, and their possible significance, and he carefully steered us in important directions, supporting the theme we were discovering in our reporting: namely that the Watergate burglary was not an isolated event, but part of a sweeping pattern of illegal, undercover activities aimed at perceived Nixon enemies—anti–Vietnam War leaders, members of the news media, Democrats, dissenters within the administration, and eventually those in the American justice system and FBI who were investigating Watergate.

Many of the old FBI memos in the files I read that day, which recorded the Bureau's progress on its investigation of Watergate, were not even written on FBI or Justice Department letterhead. Instead, they are on the blandest, garden-variety paper called Optional Form No. 10 with "United States Government, MEMORANDUM" printed at the top.

One such MEMORANDUM, dated February 21, 1973, caught my eye. "On page 1 of the Washington Post today is an article by Bob Woodward and Carl Bernstein captioned, 'Hunt Linked to Dita Beard Challenge.' (Copy attached.)"

This was during the darkest days of our Watergate coverage, eight months after the break-in, a month after Nixon's second inaugural. He had won an overwhelming election victory. Carl and I had written dozens of Watergate stories describing White House funding and involvement, but many of our colleagues in the media—even some of our fellow journalists in the *Post* newsroom—did not believe most of what we had reported.

Carl and I were scrambling hard to show that Howard Hunt, who had been a White House consultant and was the operational chief of the Watergate break-in and bugging effort, along with Gordon Liddy, a former FBI agent, had undertaken additional unsavory tasks for the White House. Having established the theme of our coverage— that undercover and illegal operations were widespread— we were beating the bushes hard to find any evidence that the Watergate burglary and the bugging operation were part of a larger campaign of secret actions designed to spy on, sabotage or do harm to political enemies. In the February 21, 1973, story we reported that Hunt had been dispatched to interview Dita Beard, a Washington lobbyist for International Telephone and Telegraph (ITT), the previous year.

Beard had been at the center of one of the biggest pre-Watergate Nixon scandals. She had written a memo alleging a connection between ITT's promise of a $400,000 contribution to the Republican convention and a favorable antitrust settlement with Nixon's Justice Department. Columnist Jack Anderson had published the Beard memo four months before Watergate, sending shock waves through the Nixon White House. In February 1973, Carl and I reported that Howard Hunt had been sent to interview Beard to attempt to demonstrate that the famous memo was a forgery, and perhaps even to get her to disavow it. A former CIA operative, Hunt had worn an ill-fitting red wig during the interview in order to disguise his identity.

But the FBI memo contained some tantalizing assertions. "As you know, Woodward and Bernstein have written numerous articles about Watergate. While their stories have contained much fiction and half truths . . ."—a favorite White House line about our Watergate stories—"they have frequently set forth information which they attribute to Federal investigators, Department of Justice sources and FBI sources. We know that they were playing games with the case agent in the Washington Field Office trying to trick him into giving them bits of information."

The memo added, "On balance and despite the fiction, there is no question but that they have access to sources either in the FBI or in the Department of Justice."

The memo said that Acting FBI Director L. Patrick Gray III had ordered that an analysis of the latest article be done immediately "to determine those portions which could have come from FBI sources and in such instances to set forth the persons having access to that particular bit of information." Six specifics were listed. The final sentence said simply, "Expedite."

The signature was one letter, a distinctive and familiar one within the Bureau hierarchy. It looked like this:

The "F" was the initial of W. Mark Felt, the acting associate director of the FBI, at the time the No. 2 position in the Bureau.

My head was swimming after I had finished the memo. W. Mark Felt was Deep Throat.

What had been going on? I wondered. This was not possible. Why would Felt initiate what amounted to a leak investigation? Fruitless as such investigations almost always are, why light the fuse? Was he just following orders? Clearly Gray had "instructed" that such an analysis be conducted. But then I realized that I had never talked with Deep Throat about that particular story. It had come from other sources outside the FBI.

Was he so clever? Possibly that clever? I read on into the files. In the FBI of 1973, expedite meant "Expedite!"

A four-page memo was ready for Acting Director Gray to see that very day. He neatly initialed it, noting the date and time, 5:07 P.M. Before it had reached Gray, however, the memo had gone to Felt, who had circled the last paragraph, which read: "As a matter of interest concerning the possible source of this article, the following information was received by Special Agent Lano (that day) from Assistant U.S. Attorney Campbell"—one of the three prosecutors working the Watergate case at the time. "Mr. Campbell advised that late yesterday, 2/20/73, reporter Woodward contacted Mr. Campbell, said he had a source of information at the White House and 'ran' the essence of the article past Mr. Campbell. Mr. Campbell told SA Lano he made no comment concerning Woodward's story."

Under the circled paragraph Felt had written in neat uppercase script: "LAST PAGE OF ATTACHED MEMO— HERE IS ENTIRE ANSWER."

Signed:

Under Felt's initial, Gray had directed that a memo be prepared for the attorney general, essentially fobbing the leak off on Campbell or the White House.

I was impressed. My guy knew his stuff. The memo was an effective cover for him, the very best counterintelligence tradecraft. Not only had he initiated the leak inquiry, but Felt appeared to have discovered the leaker.

In February 1973, it looked like Watergate was going to disappear. Nixon had been reelected; he claimed peace was at hand in Vietnam, the 16-day trial of the Watergate burglary team and Hunt and Liddy had led to guilty pleas or convictions, but there was no proof, no intimation that higher-ups were involved. Chief burglar James W. McCord Jr., the former CIA employee and Nixon campaign security chief, had not yet written his letter to Judge John Sirica, who presided over the Watergate burglary trial, exposing the perjury, the White House cover-up, and payments to the burglars for their silence.

As I read the FBI memo I wondered what the hell; was this a clever, careful protective step by Deep Throat? I had to consider the dark possibility that at that time, the man who had skillfully guided our reporting was jumping ship, having decided that unraveling Watergate was not possible. Clearly, Felt was ambitious and wanted to be named FBI director. But that very month, February 1973, Nixon had named Pat Gray the permanent director, a post the president had given him after Hoover's death, the month before Watergate. That meant a confirmation hearing before the Senate Judiciary Committee, which would doubtless probe the Bureau's Watergate investigation.

At this time, February 1973, I had an unusual meeting with Deep Throat. At his suggestion we met at a bar in Prince George's County. His message that night was that the president was on a rampage about news leaks and planned to step up his efforts to track them down and stop the media. But Felt was very relaxed that evening, suggesting that the Nixon administration was on the ropes. "They're hiding things that will come out and even discredit their war against leaks." He spoke with unusual confidence. "They can't stop the real story from coming out. That's why they're so desperate." Felt said that Pat Gray had pressured the White House into naming him to the permanent FBI directorship. Gray and former White House counsel John Dean later strongly denied this.

Over the next month, at his confirmation hearings before the Senate Judiciary Committee, Gray publicly released FBI files that substantiated some of the Watergate reports that Carl and I had written the previous year—stories that had been heatedly denied by the White House. Most significantly, the FBI files bolstered several of our major stories from the previous year—that Herbert Kalmbach, Nixon's personal lawyer, had paid Donald Segretti, who had run many of the Nixon campaign dirty-trick operations. The files also showed that Segretti had been hired by Dwight Chapin, Nixon's appointments secretary.

This public vindication relieved about 10 months of mounting frustration at the *Post*, as Carl and I recounted in *All the President's Men*. Our story in the *Post* after this disclosure was packed like a triple-ax murder. Leading the paper under a three-column headline: "FBI Chief Says/Nixon's Aides/Paid Segretti," the story was accompanied by oversized pictures of Chapin, Kalmbach and Segretti.

Soon Gray testified that John Dean "probably" lied when he told the FBI right after the Watergate burglary that he did not know Howard Hunt had a White House office.

Watergate was about to explode. For the next 18 months the daily, graphic unraveling proceeded, including the Senate Watergate hearings, televised live by all the networks, former Nixon White House aide Alexander P. Butterfield's disclosure of the secret Nixon White House tapes before that committee, the appointment and firing of Special Watergate Prosecutor Archibald Cox, the hiring of Leon Jaworski to replace Cox and continue the criminal investigation, the House Judiciary Committee impeachment investigation, the Supreme Court's unanimous decision ordering Nixon to turn over his tapes, and finally Nixon's resignation on August 9, 1974.

The revelations, the memoirs, and each season's release of a new batch of Nixon tapes continued unabated until Nixon's death in 1994 and beyond. But the mystery of Deep Throat, who had become a metaphor for the secret insider blowing the whistle, only grew with the years. Who was he? Why had he talked? And why had the secret been kept for so long? And why was I still in pursuit? What were the missing pieces of the story for me?

2

IN THE SUMMER OF 1969 I WAS SERVING AS A FULL lieutenant in the United States Navy, assigned to the Pentagon as a watch officer overseeing worldwide Teletype communications for the chief of naval operations, then Admiral Thomas H. Moorer, who later became the chairman of the Joint Chiefs of Staff, the No. 1 military position. I had a Top Secret security clearance and access to what was then called SPECAT, Special Category messages of unusual sensitivity. In addition I had a Top Secret Crypto clearance for cryptographic information on communications codes. But I had no special access to intelligence matters, which were handled over separate communications channels. My work was routine and boring. It basically involved watch-standing in the Pentagon for eight-hour shifts overseeing the communications involving the chief of naval operations, the secretary of the navy, the Navy staff and personal communications among the admirals. I disliked it.

It has been alleged in several books that my duties involved briefing Alexander M. Haig Jr., then deputy to Henry Kissinger, Nixon's national security adviser, in the White House. Thus a number of people, at first including John Dean, speculated incorrectly that Haig was Deep Throat. I'm certain I never met or talked to Haig until years later. But as Admiral Moorer has said publicly and repeatedly, I acted at times as a courier, taking packages of messages or other documents (they were in sealed envelopes, so I rarely knew what was inside) to the White House.

One evening I was dispatched with such a package to the lower level of the West Wing of the White House, where there was a little waiting room near the Situation Room and the offices of some National Security Council staff. I vaguely recall there were several vending machines nearby or down the hall. It was approaching dinnertime or later. It could be a long wait to get the proper person to come out and sign for the material, an hour or more. But I was fascinated by the White House—it sure beat the Pentagon—and, when there were such opportunities, I hung around as much as possible. I was delighted to wait.

The mystique of the White House is compelling. Just

being there was its own reward with the suggestion that important business was transpiring nearby.

I might have volunteered to bring the papers that evening after a routine watch. It was either in the last quarter of 1969 but probably the first half of 1970 as best I can tell. I am pretty sure I was in my dress-blue Navy uniform, the formal suit with two gold stripes and a star on each sleeve, which is worn in the colder months. So I was 26 or had just turned 27. My hair was close-cropped as required by the Navy. The White House was and still is often full of people in military uniforms, bustling about or waiting.

Roger Morris, an aide to Henry Kissinger, has suggested that I was a briefer for Haig, but the only evidence Morris has offered is that he saw me sitting outside the NSC offices in the West Wing during this period. He is right in that I was there. But I never briefed Haig.

After waiting some time that evening, a tall man with perfectly combed gray hair came in and sat down to wait. His suit was dark, his shirt was white, and his necktie subdued. He was probably 25 to 30 years older than I. He too carried a file case or a briefcase. He was distinguished-looking and had a studied air of confidence, even what might be called a command presence, the posture and calm of someone used to giving orders and having them obeyed instantly and without question. He had an air of patience and comfort about him. I could tell he was observing the situation carefully. There was nothing over-bearing in his attentiveness, but it was evident because his eyes were darting about—a gentlemanly surveillance.

After several minutes, I introduced myself. "Lieutenant Bob Woodward," I said, carefully appending a deferential "sir."

"Mark Felt," he said. He had a great, confident voice. Here was authority. He offered no details about himself. He seemed tightly wound but accustomed to waiting in situations like this. As best I can recall I thought he was either delivering something important or waiting for an appointment. His shoes were well shined but not a military shine, and his hair was slightly long for any of the services.

I remember trying to probe by talking about myself. I told him that this was my last year in the Navy and that I was bringing documents from Admiral Moorer's office. Felt was in no hurry to explain anything about himself or his presence.

This was a time in my life of considerable anxiety, even consternation, about my future. I had been involuntarily extended an additional year in the Navy because of the Vietnam War, having already served four years after college. I had graduated in 1965 from Yale, where I had a Naval Reserve Officer Training Corps (NROTC) scholarship that required I go into the Navy after getting my degree.

During that year in Washington, I expended a great deal of energy to find things or people who were interesting. I had a college classmate who was going to clerk for Chief Justice Warren Burger, and I made an effort to develop a friendship with him. To quell my angst and the sense of drift I was taking graduate courses at George Washington University. One course was in Shakespeare and another in international relations. I mentioned this graduate work at GW, as George Washington was commonly called, to Felt.

He perked up immediately, saying he had attended night law school at GW in the 1930s before joining—and this is the first time he mentioned it—the FBI. While attending night law school, he said, he had worked full-time for his home state senator from Idaho.

I mentioned that I had been doing some volunteer work at the office of my congressman, John Erlenborn, a Republican from the district in Wheaton, Illinois, where I had been raised.

So, I thought, we had two connections—graduate work at GW and work with elected representatives from our home states.

Felt and I were like two passengers sitting next to each other on a long airline flight with nowhere to go and nothing really to do but resign ourselves to the dead time. He showed no interest in striking up a long conversation. I was intent on it. I finally extracted information that he was an assistant director of the FBI in charge of the inspection division, an important post under Director J. Edgar Hoover. That meant he led teams of agents who went around to the FBI field offices to see if they were adhering to procedures and carrying out Hoover's orders. I later learned this was called the "goon squad."

I am sure I was almost drooling, way too anxious and curious. Here was someone at the center of the secret world I was only glimpsing in my Navy assignment. My incessant questions, I recall, didn't elicit much more information. So I talked about myself. I had managed during this period to get an interview with former Secretary of State Dean Acheson for a paper I was doing in the international relations course at GW. I recall during this first encounter—or perhaps a later one—recounting to Felt how I had gone to see Acheson at Covington & Burling, his old law firm where he still had an office. The old Cold Warrior did not disappoint me in the interview, colorfully describing George Kennan, the renowned author of the containment doctrine, whom Acheson considered to be softer on the Communists than he. Kennan, Acheson said, was like an old horse pulling a buggy over a bridge who would stop periodically to see if it was he who was making all the noise.

Whether it was a person or a book or an idea, I grabbed on to it, often too hard, even fiercely. So too with Mark Felt, obviously a man of immense experience and rank in the FBI, but now my captive audience. I peppered him with questions about his job and the world. The wait was long but seemed shorter as I probed. Getting nowhere with him, I shared my ambitions. I had written a full-length novel in college that was neither promising nor publishable, though I still had hopes. Maybe I would try to become a novelist, I said, or a college professor, teaching English or political science. Maybe I would become a lawyer like him or my father. My father had graduated from Northwestern Law School in the 1930s. Felt and my father were the same age, both born in 1913.

As I think back on this accidental but crucial encounter—one of the most important in my life—I see that my patter verged on the adolescent. But Felt had no choice. I turned it into a career counseling session. Since he wasn't saying much about himself, I became a parody of the cliché—enough about me, what do you think of me? What should I do? I recall that Felt said he had a daughter my age who had gone to Stanford.

I've tried to establish the date of this first encounter but I can't be sure. It is possible that Felt was there to see someone about what was then the Nixon administration's highly secret program that tapped the telephones of 17 journalists and White House aides. The telephone tapping was designed, at least in part, to track down officials who were leaking national security information to reporters. Records from the Watergate investigation later revealed that the FBI sent 37 letters to Dr. Kissinger reporting on the results of the various electronic surveillances from May 13, 1969, to May 11, 1970. Perhaps Felt was just bringing one of those Top Secret letters which had to have been handled very carefully, and were probably delivered by courier. Felt later denied that he knew of the Kissinger wiretaps at this time.

Years later, the 17 wiretaps were among the most controversial of the Watergate revelations. Those whose phones were tapped included William Safire, a Nixon White House speechwriter and later the *New York Times* columnist, and Anthony Lake, a top Kissinger aide who later resigned over the invasion of Cambodia and who eventually served as President Bill Clinton's national security adviser. The military assistant to Secretary of Defense Melvin Laird, who often clashed with Kissinger, also had his phones tapped as part of the program, which was carried out by the FBI.

But all of that and much, much more was unknown, even unimaginable, as I sat there with Felt. I continued to engage him in conversation; mostly my questions and uneasy expressions about my future, the subject that haunted me. I was deferential, though I must have seemed needy. He was friendly and I interpreted that to mean he was paternal. Still the most vivid impression I have is of his distant, formal manner, a product of Hoover's FBI. I asked for Felt's phone number and he gave me the direct line to his FBI office.

I believe I encountered him only one more time at the White House. But I had set the hook. He was going to be one of the people I consulted in depth about my future—still the subject of my confusion and uncertainty as the much anticipated date of my discharge from the Navy approached in August 1970.

At some point I called him, first at the FBI and then at his home in Virginia. I was a little desperate, and I'm sure I poured out my heart. I had applied to several law schools, hoping to be accepted for the fall of 1970. Now 27, I wondered if I should—or how I could stand—spending three years in law school before starting real work.

Somewhat sympathetic to the lost-soul quality of my questions, Felt told me that after he had his law degree his first job had been with the Federal Trade Commission. This was the early 1940s, when he was in his late 20s. His first assignment was to determine for the FTC if toilet paper with the Red Cross brand name had an unfair competitive advantage because people thought it was endorsed or approved by the American Red Cross. People were resistant to questions about their toilet paper usage, he discovered, and he couldn't solve the case. The FTC was a classic federal bureaucracy, slow and leaden, and he hated it. Go with the action, he said. Within a year he had applied to the FBI and been accepted. The training was grueling, almost around-the-clock. But then the work as an agent and supervisor centered on important, unsolved cases, crimes or mysteries. He thought law school opened the most doors, but find your heart, he said in so many words. Don't get caught in your own personal equivalent of the Federal Trade Commission toilet paper investigation.

It seemed like a nearly perfect metaphor for the pitfalls I might face—in some ways, as I recall, a revelation. I was thankful for the advice. Even now decades later, I consider his advice a kind of "Rosebud," the elusive X-factor in someone's life that explains everything. The Rosebud here was the realization that I was free to choose. The Navy was the opposite, and I had to be careful that I didn't sign up for someone else's plan for my life. My father, who had been a partner in a law firm in Illinois, wanted me to go to law school and eventually join the firm. School and the Navy were so programmed. But I could choose. I was on a binge of applications and interviews considering the broadest range of possible jobs or careers. I even sent off for an application to the Central Intelligence Agency but never applied because the forms seemed long and complicated. And wouldn't it be too much like the Navy? I set up interviews with businesses, including Procter & Gamble, which hired young people to manage the marketing of their products, everything from soap to toothpaste. A girlfriend joked that I could become "Mr. Jiffy Peanut Butter," the man in charge of selling sandwich spread. Of course there were law school applications and I was finally accepted.

I reported the good news to all, including Felt, who seemed glad I had not applied to the CIA and would not be marketing peanut butter or the like.

On the Friday before I was due to be discharged, the Navy commander who was technically my boss (I think his last name was Kingston) and some of my Navy colleagues threw a party for me at one of the officers clubs in Virginia. Martinis were about 90 cents, if that, and I believe I had maybe even six or seven—more alcohol than I had ever consumed at one time, before or since. I was so drunk and sick sitting in the back of Kingston's car that I remember throwing up on the floor, definitely not the protocol, even for an officer leaving the naval service. I recall Kingston's wife, sitting in the front seat, barely able to contain her disgust. Earlier Kingston, who wrote my fitness reports, the Navy's regular six-month officer evaluations, said that I had been operating on only one or two of my eight cylinders in the Navy and he genuinely hoped I would find something to engage more of them. He dropped me—dumped me— in something like the north parking lot at the Pentagon, where my car, a Volkswagen Beetle, was parked.

I couldn't walk and began crawling. Military police came to investigate who was crawling around the parking lot. I showed them my identification, and noted that I was out of the Navy or nearly out. We called it "short"—meaning only a few days to go. The police were sympathetic, perhaps jealous, and indicated that a short-timer was entitled to one binge. They or one of my colleagues drove me back to my apartment in the District of Columbia. I lived in a $110-a-month efficiency on the sixth floor, No. 617 of 1718 P Street Northwest, near Dupont Circle.

I have never again known the equivalent of the next morning's headache—continuous and throbbing. It must be what a migraine is like. To this day, I can't drink or smell a martini without feeling vaguely sick.

I was formally discharged and I had August of 1970 to myself, and I went prowling. Law school seemed gutless. I had had a gutless five years in the Navy. I detested the Vietnam War, but never did anything about it other than march in an antiwar protest in D.C.

I subscribed to *The Washington Post*, which I knew was led by a colorful, hard-charging editor named Ben Bradlee. There was a toughness and edge to the coverage that I liked; it seemed to fit the times, to fit with a general sense of where the world was, much more than law school. Maybe reporting was something I could do.

3

DURING MY SCRAMBLE FOR A FUTURE, I HAD sent a letter to the *Post* asking for a job as a reporter. Somehow—I don't remember exactly how—Harry Rosenfeld, the metropolitan editor, agreed to see me.

It is quite likely that I just showed up at the paper that day to track down Rosenfeld. This was before today's tight security and anyone could literally walk into the paper and go to the fifth-floor newsroom. The *Post,* at 15th and L Streets Northwest, was just a seven-block walk from my apartment at 17th and P.

In less than two years, Rosenfeld would be one of the key editors for the Watergate stories that Bernstein and I did. Rosenfeld, who was in his early 40s, popped antacid tablets and had the nervousness and unrelenting intensity of a man with a stomach condition. Born in pre-Nazi Berlin, he had come to New York City at the age of 10. In *All the President's Men,* Bernstein and I said that Rosenfeld ran the metropolitan staff, the *Post's* largest, like a football coach. We wrote, "He prods his players, letting them know that he has promised the front office results, pleading, yelling, cajoling, pacing, working his facial expressions for instant effects—anger, satisfaction, concern."

That day in August 1970, he put much of this on display in his small office. With his tie loose, he stared through his glasses at me in some bewilderment. Why, he wondered, would I want to be a reporter? I had zero—zero!—experience. Why, he asked, would *The Washington Post* want to hire someone with no experience? He reached for a stack of files. These were applicants to work at the *Post,* he said. Stacks—everyone, nearly everyone, wanted to work at the *Post.* He shuffled through the files. Here was someone with a full five years' experience on a big, important paper in the Midwest who was begging, dying to be hired. He found someone with ten years' experience. Ten years. Someone else on the doorstep had won all kinds of journalism prizes. Why you? he asked.

I didn't have much of an answer, and I recall only that I fumbled through, mentioning something about experiment and desire.

He asked me what "attribution" was.

I don't know, I said.

He wagged his head and explained that it meant every-thing in the newspaper had to be attributed—the mayor said, or the document shows, or a source said. The reader had to know the basis for everything as close as possible.

Rosenfeld was so aghast at my ignorance, which was even greater than my arrogance, this boldness, this pre-sumptuousness, that he motioned some of his editors over. He flailed his arms in the air, essentially saying, Look at this guy, he wants to work here as a reporter and he has zero experience. He didn't even work on his college news-paper!

I think I had included a copy of my graduate course paper on Dean Acheson. Rosenfeld pronounced it irrelevant, ab-solutely irrelevant to journalism, and tossed it aside. Given his mood, I could imagine him throwing it on the floor and stomping on it.

This is just crazy enough, Rosenfeld finally said, revers-ing field, that we ought to try it. We'll give you a two-week tryout, he said, and assigned me to report to his deputy, Andrew Barnes, a personable Harvard graduate who later went on to be editor and CEO of the St. Petersburg Times in Florida.

Barnes had a desk in the middle of the newsroom. He looked at me in mild exasperation as if to say, another of Harry's experiments. Barnes kind of slumped forward and looked like a senior CIA case officer who had been told to run a blind man (me) to read enemy maps.

My first assignment, Barnes said, was a local story on gas stations. After a spate of nighttime robberies, several gas stations had instituted a policy of exact change at night, meaning that customers had to pay cash, which was deposited through a slit in the top of a large safe that could not be opened by the night shift. With no cash on hand, robberies would stop.

I was absolutely enthralled with the possibilities as I left the building.

I recall walking back to my apartment, realizing that I could go to every gas station in town as a *Post* reporter, and probe every angle in this new crime-stopping tactic that surely was sweeping Washington and the suburbs. I probably visited dozens of gas stations, but I only found two that were using the exact change safes. Two days later I reported to Barnes.

You saw *The New York Times,* didn't you? he asked.

No. I didn't read *The New York Times.*

You ought to, he said, scoffing. He threw the paper at me. A large article on their metropolitan front page described the use of exact change in filling stations in New York.

I had been scooped on my first assignment. Barnes's face said: I have lost confidence in you. I was crushed. I apologized. He gave me a few more assignments and I tried to come up with some stories of my own. After two weeks, I had written perhaps a dozen stories or fragments of stories. None had been published or come close to being published. None had even been edited.

See, you don't know how to do this, Rosenfeld said, bringing my tryout to a merciful close. If you're serious, he said, and I'm not sure you are serious at all, get a job at a small newspaper and learn the basics. He said there was a small but respected weekly newspaper in the Maryland suburbs, *The Montgomery County Sentinel*. The editor, Roger Farquhar, had once been the state editor at the *Post* and he knew how to train reporters.

I left more enthralled than ever. Though I had failed the tryout completely—it was a spectacular crash—I realized I had found something that I loved. The sense of immediacy in a newsroom and the newspaper was overwhelming to me. I called Roger Farquhar, applied for one of his four reporting jobs, and went to an interview at the *Sentinel*'s offices in downtown Rockville, Maryland, nearly an hour northwest of D.C. in the Maryland suburbs.

Farquhar, a heavy-smoking, brilliant and profoundly skeptical editor, later said he had hired me because I said, "I want this job so bad I can taste it." That was how I felt, and I'm sure I said it. I informed my father that law school was off and that I was taking a job, at about $115 a week, as a reporter at a weekly newspaper in Maryland.

"You're crazy," my father said in one of the rare judgmental statements he had ever made to me.

I also called Mark Felt, who in a gentler way also indicated that this was crazy. He said he thought newspapers were too shallow and too quick on the draw. Newspapers didn't do in-depth work and rarely got to the bottom of events.

Well, I said, I was elated. Maybe he could help me with stories.

He didn't answer, I recall.

THE YEAR AT THE SENTINEL was an education. Roger Farquhar gave me the freedom to pursue minor investigative stories, and I did several that the Post had to follow. One story I did on black militant H. Rap Brown reported that a state prosecutor told me arson charges against Brown had been "fabricated." The prosecutor stuck to his story and the Post and The New York Times followed my reporting with front page stories of their own.

During that year, I kept in touch with Felt through phone calls to his office or home. We were becoming friends of a sort. He was the mentor, keeping me from toilet paper investigations, and I was the understudy who kept asking for advice and kept the questions coming. I could get him on the phone and keep him there for 10 to 20 minutes. One weekend I drove out to his home in Virginia and met his wife, Audrey.

Somewhat to my astonishment, I found that Felt was an admirer of J. Edgar Hoover. He appreciated the orderliness of Hoover, who ran the Bureau with rigid procedures and an iron fist. Hoover was always well dressed, fresh and direct. Felt said he appreciated that Hoover arrived at the office at 6:30 each morning and that everyone knew what was expected. The Nixon White House was another matter, Felt said. The political pressures were immense, he said, without providing any specifics. I believe he called it corrupt and sinister. Hoover, Felt and the old guard were the wall that protected the FBI, he said.

In his own memoir, *The FBI Pyramid*, which received almost no attention when it was published in 1979, five years after Nixon's resignation, Felt angrily denounced the effort to assert political control of the FBI through what he called a "White House–Justice Department cabal."

At the time, in the 1970–71 pre-Watergate period, there was little public knowledge of the vast pushing, shoving and acrimony between the White House and the FBI. For example, as the Watergate investigations later revealed, in 1970 a young White House aide named Tom Charles Huston came up with a plan to authorize the CIA, FBI and military intelligence units to intensify electronic surveillance of "domestic security threats," to authorize illegal opening of mail, and lift the restrictions on surreptitious entries or break-ins to gather intelligence. Huston warned in a Top Secret memo that the plan was "clearly illegal." President Nixon initially approved the plan. Hoover strenuously objected, principally because eavesdropping, opening mail and breaking into homes and offices of domestic security threats was basically the FBI baili-wick and they didn't want competition. Four days later Nixon rescinded the Huston plan.

Felt later wrote that he considered Huston himself "a kind of White House gauleiter over the intelligence community." The four-inch-thick *Webster's Encyclopedic Unabridged Dictionary* defines a gauleiter as "the leader or chief official of a political district under Nazi control."

There is little doubt what Felt thought of the Nixon team. During this period, he also stopped efforts by some in the Bureau to "identify every member of every hippie com-mune" in the Los Angeles area, for example, or to open a file on every member of the Students for a Democratic Society.

"This was an utterly ridiculous proposal," Felt wrote. "In the first place, only a very small number of members had actually advocated or participated in violence and there was no justification for investigating others." It would involve opening thousands of new cases and the FBI didn't have the manpower, he added.

None of this surfaced directly in our discussions, but it was clear to me that he was a man under pressure. The threat to the integrity and independence of the Bureau was real and uppermost in his mind.

On July 1, 1971—about a year before both Hoover's death and the Watergate break-in—Hoover promoted Felt to be the No. 3 in the FBI. Though Hoover's sidekick, Clyde Tolson, was technically the No. 2, Tolson was ill and didn't come to work many days, meaning he didn't have operational control of the Bureau. That meant my friend Mark Felt became the day-to-day manager of all FBI matters as long as he kept Hoover and Tolson informed or received Hoover's approval on policy matters. It was during this period that Felt was being flooded with calls from Nixon White House aides requesting political information, small and large favors.

Right at this time, August 1971, a year after my failed tryout at the *Post*, Rosenfeld finally decided to hire me. I went to the *Post* on what I recall was the first Friday of September 1971 for my final interviews, including a meeting with Bradlee.

As best I can reconstruct it was Friday, September 3, 1971. Unbeknownst to us at the time, of course, within 24 hours of my meeting with Bradlee, White House aide Howard Hunt would lead a burglary team to Los Angeles to break into the office of the psychiatrist to Daniel Ellsberg, who had leaked the Pentagon Papers to *The New York Times*. Hunt and his sidekick, Liddy, the so-called Plumbers, were working to stop news leaks, in part because the White House did not believe it could count on the FBI to tackle the leaks aggressively. The previous month, on August 11, 1971, John D. Ehrlichman, one of Nixon's two top aides and chief domestic adviser, had checked "Approved" on a memo recommending that "a covert operation be undertaken to examine all the medical files still held by Ellsberg's psychoanalyst." Ehrlichman had added in his own hand, "if done under your assurance that it is not traceable."

Bradlee was not interested in what I had done at what he called "the Montgomery County whatever-it-is newspaper." He was notorious for a short attention span, but when he turned his face and eyes and his undivided focus on you, he conveyed the sense you had arrived. He homed in on one thing: my time in the Navy. My five years had not been hard war years like his own service during World War II on a tin can, the destroyer USS *Philip,* but even across a generation, we were a band of brothers of sorts. Everything after the Navy was easy, we agreed. Well, get to work, enjoy yourself, have fun and dig, he said.

I started at the *Post* on September 15, 1971. The pay was $165 a week. Because the union gave me no credit for reporting experience at a weekly newspaper—only daily experience counted—I was the lowest-paid reporter. I was assigned the night police reporter slot, roughly from 6:30 P.M. to 2 A.M. the next day. To many it was the worst assignment. I loved it. Fires, shootings, investigations, the gritty and shocking street crimes, and the politics of the police department were all subjects where I could find stories. I loved newspapering so much that I often worked the day shift also.

Don Graham, the son of Katharine Graham, the publisher and owner of the *Post*, came by my desk one day during this period. Don, who would later become publisher and CEO, had been a local editor and reporter and would work at nearly every job on the business side. He mentioned that someone from the union was complaining that I was working more than the prescribed $37^1/_2$ hours a week without putting in for overtime. As I recall, Don only smiled and gave me an encouraging wink or slap on the shoulder.

At the FBI, unknown to the public or to me, in early 1972 Felt was under what he would later call "White House pressure to take part in a cover-up which in some ways was a prelude to Watergate." It was more than a prelude; it was a dress rehearsal, suggesting that White House pressure on the FBI could limit an investigation.

It was on February 19, 1972, that columnist Jack Anderson published the Dita Beard memo suggesting that ITT had made the $400,000 donation to the Republicans in exchange for a favorable antitrust settlement. John Mitchell had resigned as attorney general to run the Nixon 1972 reelection campaign and his deputy Richard G. Kleindienst had been nominated by Nixon to move up to attorney general.

Patrick Gray, then an assistant attorney general, was in charge of shepherding the Kleindienst nomination through the Senate.

Although it was later overshadowed by Watergate, ITT was a big scandal at the time. On March 10, 1972, Gray called Felt at the FBI and told him he wanted to meet on an urgent matter. Hoover was still alive then. Gray was the head of the Justice Department's civil division, and he almost certainly never imagined he would succeed Hoover at the FBI.

At the time, Felt had never met Gray, a former World War II submarine commander who was nearly six feet tall with a military haircut. Gray brought the original of the Beard memo. He wanted Felt to have the FBI lab determine if it was authentic. Felt took the memo from Gray, and obtained clearance from Hoover to proceed with the document examination. But soon Gray was on the phone, insisting that the document be returned at once.

Four days later Gray returned the memo to the FBI for the lab tests. Because he had no known typewriter specimens for comparison, however, the lab could reach no positive conclusions.

Soon Felt received a call from White House counsel John Dean saying that the experts ITT had brought in determined the memo was a forgery because examination showed it had been typed six months after it was dated.

So on March 17, Dita Beard, who was suspiciously in the hospital, perhaps to keep her under wraps, issued a statement saying of the memo, "I did not prepare it and could not have. . . ."

The FBI lab, however, reported to Felt that they believed the memo had been typed on or about the date on the memo—June 2, 1971—and that it was probably authentic.

Dean then urged Felt to change an FBI letter reporting this finding to make it innocuous or at least not to conflict with the ITT finding. Felt and Hoover refused.

"Felt would not budge, because the director would not budge," Dean wrote later in his memoir, *Blind Ambition*. Even a note from President Nixon to Hoover failed to persuade the director, according to Dean.

For Felt, it was White House pressure to cover up, pure and simple.

THOUGH I WAS BUSY at the *Post* in the early months, I checked in with Felt regularly. He was relatively open with me but insisted that he, the FBI and the Justice Department be kept out of anything I might write or pass on to others at the paper. He was stern and strict about those rules, which he issued with a booming, insistent voice. I promised. He said that it was essential I be careful. The only way to ensure total confidentiality was that I tell no one—no one—that we knew each other or had talked, or that I knew anyone in the

FBI or Justice. That spring he told me in utter confidence that the FBI had information that Vice President Spiro T. Agnew had received a bribe of $2,500 in cash that he had put in his desk drawer.

I passed this on to Richard Cohen, then the top Maryland reporter for the *Post*. I did not identify the source at all. Cohen said and later wrote in his book on the Agnew investigation that he had thought it was "preposterous." I recall that another *Post* reporter and I spent a day chasing around Baltimore for the person who allegedly knew about the bribe. We got nowhere. Two years later, the Agnew investigation revealed that the vice president had indeed received such a bribe in his office.

4
___

ABOUT 9:45 A.M. ON TUESDAY, MAY 2, 1972, FELT was in his office at the Bureau when an assistant director came to report that Director J. Edgar Hoover had died at his home. Felt was shocked. For practical purposes he was next in line to take over the FBI.

To understand Felt it is necessary to understand his relationship with Hoover. "I felt no sense of personal loss," Felt wrote in his book and then devotes a 15-page chapter to defending Hoover, whom he characterized as "charismatic, feisty, charming, petty, giant, grandiose, brilliant, egotistical, industrious, formidable, compassionate, domineering."

As he reviewed Hoover's career, Felt's account is respectful of this ultimate authority figure, but there is also a sense that he never grew close to or knew the man other than through their formal communications. Felt seems to have been knocking on Hoover's door in an effort to know him better, to get closer, but Hoover's only personal relationship was with Tolson. Felt says that he had no knowledge that Hoover, a lifelong bachelor, might have had a homosexual relationship with Tolson or anyone else. He describes Hoover as stubborn and inflexible on such matters as typographical errors and his rigid insistence that incoming letters from outside the Bureau be answered within 24 hours. Every phone call was to be answered by the third ring.

But Felt goes to great lengths to put Hoover's career in the most positive light, pointing out that after Pearl Harbor, for example, Hoover was the one senior official who opposed the relocation and internment of Japanese-American citizens. In Felt's words, Hoover was "the one man of high rank in the federal government who sought to prevent this rape of the Constitution and of human rights."

Many people would find it laughable to see Hoover described as a defender of the Constitution and human rights. Yet in a long chapter on the Bureau's wiretapping of the Reverend Martin Luther King Jr. in the 1960s, Felt goes so far as to justify Hoover's actions and blames others, including Attorney General Robert F. Kennedy, who Felt says was worried by King's ties to a member of the Communist Party. The King investigation, according to Felt, "demonstrates the stresses and strains under which the FBI operated." Felt noted that in addition to telephone taps, "microphones were placed in various hotel and motel rooms occupied by Dr. King in his travels about the United States."

In Felt's telling, it is almost King's fault that Hoover had to learn the details of King's private life. "When the puritanical Director read the transcripts of the tapes disclosing what went on behind Dr. King's closed hotel doors," Felt wrote, "he was outraged by the drunken sexual orgies, including acts of perversion often involving several persons.

"What the tapes recorded was a running account of [King's] extramarital sex life. On his journey about the country in quest of civil rights, he had been visited in his hotel rooms by a parade of white females, and it was all there to be heard, right down to his outcries in the throes of passion. Frequently his male visitors joined in the festivities."

Felt writes approvingly of Hoover's campaign to discredit King because King was, in the director's eyes, a hypocrite who did not have the morality to head the civil rights movement. The ends justified the means. Using that information was permissible for a larger, worthy purpose, and a judgment that could be made outside the law.

PERHAPS FELT TOLERATED my aggressiveness and pushy approach because he had been the same way when he was a junior FBI supervisor in Seattle. After a dozen years as an agent, Felt wrangled a 30-minute, one-on-one meeting with Hoover. By Felt's account, he had laid out his ambitions to the director. "Mr. Hoover," he said, "I feel ready for more responsibility. My ambition is to be a Special Agent in Charge. I feel confident I can handle the job whenever you feel I am ready for it."

Hoover seemed pleased when Felt took copious notes about Hoover's list of FBI problems, and interjected some of his own views.

Within a week, Felt was ordered to Washington and promoted to the position of inspector's aide. The inspection staff was the FBI's internal police. Felt maintained he was not happy to join what he described as the "goon squad." But Hoover called the inspection staff his "eyes and ears" within the Bureau and Felt believed it was the only way for him to get promoted. The staff's main job was to conduct an annual inspection of each of the Bureau's field offices. A team of inspectors would sweep into town and go through every file, turning the place upside down. Only two months into his tenure, Felt was sent back out into the field offices, a transfer that did not displease him. But 10 years later, Hoover again brought Felt back to the inspection division, this time as its chief—in other words, the chief goon. This often entailed special Hoover missions.

In 1965, for example, when there was a revolution in the

Dominican Republic, Hoover sent Felt to the scene. The Bureau was wiretapping the telephone of the chief insurgent, "the exiled former president, the leftist Juan Bosch," as Felt put it. All of the revolutionaries' strategies and plans were being sent to an eager President Lyndon Johnson. But the translated intercepts were being sent too slowly by Morse code, and the backlog of intercepts was horrendous. The FBI in Santo Domingo had an automatic encryption device, but security procedures of the National Security Agency prohibited its use from a room that was not lead-lined to prevent emissions that others might pick up.

"This is an emergency," Felt told FBI agents on the scene, "and we aren't going to worry about regulations." The Crypto machine was used, and as Felt wrote, "I had accomplished my objective—and I had done it in one day as Hoover had demanded." It should have been a CIA operation, which had responsibility for intelligence gathering overseas, and Felt notes it was the beginning of the FBI-CIA rift. But President Johnson was "very pleased."

That year, 1965, I was a young officer in the U.S. Navy assigned to a command and communications ship, the USS Wright, that served as a floating Pentagon and an alternative relocation site for the president in case of nuclear war. The Wright's official designation was NECPA—National Emergency Command Post Afloat. I was in charge of the Top Secret communications circuits and oversaw the National

Security Agency cryptographic machines. Working out of properly shielded rooms was the big security fad at the time. The TEMPEST hazard, as it was called, was the possibility that the signal from a decrypted message could be picked up by the Soviet intelligence service and then matched with the encrypted message. This could result in the Soviets breaking U.S. communications codes. Felt's decision to ignore the regulation could have been viewed as serious.

ON THE DAY OF HOOVER'S DEATH, Felt wrote, "It did not cross my mind that the President would appoint an outsider to replace Hoover. . . . My own record was good and I allowed myself to think I had an excellent chance."

He was soon to be disappointed.

"Exactly 26 hours and ten minutes after he had announced Hoover's death," Felt wrote, President Nixon nominated L. Patrick Gray to be acting director. Gray was a Nixon loyalist going back years. He had resigned from the Navy in 1960 to work for Nixon during the presidential campaign that Nixon lost to John F. Kennedy.

As best I could tell Felt was crushed but he put on a good face. Hoover's funeral was a "televised spectacular, designed more to aggrandize the President than to honor the departed Director," Felt wrote bitterly.

Pat Gray's appointment added to the bitterness. "I was

resentful that an outsider was taking over, yet at the same time, I was impressed with the strength and sincerity of this man."

Felt found it nearly impossible to get Gray's attention for more than a few minutes at a time. Gray had a habit of saying he would think about Felt's various recommendations, but that meant the acting director had already made up his mind.

Felt found Gray lying in public when Gray announced that the top FBI officials had "unanimously approved" the hiring of female agents for the first time. No vote had been taken and nearly all of the top officials were opposed.

"Had I been wiser, I would have retired," Felt wrote. "I was making pennies an hour," since his retirement take-home pay would have nearly equaled his active service salary. Gray was often out of town visiting field offices, or in the gym exercising, where he would not permit intrusions. He brought four young, loyal staffers with him from Justice. In Felt's eyes they were a menace, occupying hours of Gray's time in closed-door sessions.

ON MAY 15, 1972, less than two weeks after Hoover's death and Gray's installation as acting director, a gunman shot Alabama Governor George Wallace, then running for president, in a Maryland shopping center. The wounds were grave. Wallace lived, but his legs were paralyzed.

Wallace had a strong following in the Deep South, an increasing source of Nixon's support. Wallace's spoiler candidacy in 1968 could have cost Nixon the election that year, and Nixon had monitored Wallace's every move closely as the 1972 presidential campaign continued.

That evening Nixon called Felt at home—Gray was out of town—to get an update on the Wallace shooting. It was the first time Felt had directly spoken with the president. Felt reported that Arthur Bremer, the would-be assassin, was in custody and in the hospital because he had been roughed up by those who apprehended him.

"Well, it's too bad they didn't really rough up the son of a bitch!" Nixon said, according to Felt's book.

Felt seemed offended at this outburst. A tape of the call, however, shows Nixon less agitated, saying, "I hope they worked him over a little bit more than that." According to the tape, Felt said with a chuckle, "I think they did pretty well."

The potential political ramifications of the Wallace shooting were staggering. The segregationist Wallace was running in the Democratic primaries and he had become a national phenomenon. He had won the Florida primary two months earlier with 42 percent of the vote. The eventual Democratic nominee, Senator George McGovern, had taken only 6 percent. Nationally Nixon was at about 43 percent, with Wallace polling 10 to 12 percent. Most of Wallace's supporters would otherwise represent Nixon votes. Wallace was now out of the race, and as Theodore H. White later wrote in *The Making of the President 1972*, "with that elimination, the re-election of the president was finally, irrevocably assured." In the November election, Nixon received a stunning 61 percent to McGovern's 37 percent.

No wonder Nixon was fretful. If the shooter had any connection to Nixon, the Republicans or the White House—or merely had been a supporter—the implications could have been immense. More than a year later, Carl Bernstein and I would establish and publish a story saying that on the night of the shooting, Nixon aide Charles W. Colson ordered Howard Hunt to break into Bremer's apartment in Milwaukee to discover if Bremer had any connections to political groups, hopefully tying Bremer to left-wing politicians.

In the following days I called Felt several times. He very carefully pointed me in the right direction—gave me leads— as we at the *Post* tried to find out more about Arthur Bremer. It turned out that Bremer had stalked some of the other presidential candidates, and I went to New York City to pick up the trail. This led to several front page stories about Bremer's travels, completing a portrait of a madman who had not singled out Wallace but who was looking for any presidential candidate to shoot. On May 18, I did a front page story: "High federal officials who have reviewed investigative reports on the Wallace shooting said yesterday that there is no evidence whatsoever to indicate that Bremer was a hired killer.

"At least 200 FBI agents still were following leads across the country and have found no indication of a conspiracy in the Wallace shooting, federal sources here in Washington said."

It was rather brazen of me. Though I was technically protecting my source and had talked to others besides Felt, I was not doing an adequate job of concealing where the information was coming from. I might as well have raised a flag that said "FBI—senior official reviewing investigative reports is talking." It wasn't astute at all, and Felt chastised me mildly. But the story that Bremer had acted alone was one that both the White House and the FBI wanted out. The effort to dampen conspiracy theories basically worked, and to my knowledge it was true. No one ever seriously or effectively suggested the Wallace shooting involved others.

IN HIS EARLY DAYS AT THE FBI, Gray generated an immense amount of hostility, especially with Felt. Gray continued his program of visiting each of the FBI field offices, insisting on using expensive military aircraft—the high cost of which had to be reimbursed from the FBI budget. Gray had a private kitchen with a $10,000-a-year chef installed in his suite of offices. It was supposed to be for the top executives, who were assessed $25 each to initially stock the kitchen. They were then periodically hit up again for money. Felt was offended and calculated that he got meals there only about twice a month. Something like $12.50 for a meal, no matter how good, seemed outrageously expensive at the time.

"The immediate and most noticeable effect of the kitchen and the gourmet meals—and they were that!—was the cooking smells which filled the public corridor," Felt wrote later.

Felt said that Gray complained about the endless flow of paper. "I'm expecting you to run the day-to-day operations of the FBI," Gray told Felt, "and until I become more familiar with procedures I will not be able to handle much paperwork."

In other words, Gray got to be director of the FBI, and Felt did the work. Hoover had been founding director of the Bureau in 1924, serving an incredible 48 years, including the entire 30 years Felt had been in the Bureau. The directorship was coveted, the director almost a god. And it had been handed to Pat Gray, an FBI outsider with feet of clay who smelled up the hallways, in order to assert political control. Felt sent only about 10 percent of the paper flow to Gray but even that overwhelmed the new acting director.

At 7 A.M. Saturday, June 17, 1972, just six weeks after Hoover's death, the FBI night supervisor had something serious to report. As usual Gray was out of town, so the supervisor called Felt at home. Five men in business suits, pockets stuffed with $100 bills, and carrying eavesdropping and photographic equipment, had been arrested inside the Democrats' national headquarters at the Watergate office building earlier, at about 2:30 A.M.

"What in the world were they doing?" Felt asked.

By 8:30 A.M., he was in his office at the FBI, and calling the night supervisor for an update.

"This is getting rather complicated," the supervisor said. "I'd better come over to your office." He reported that the men were wearing surgical plastic or rubber gloves and carried at least $2,300 in cash. They were in jail, not talking at all. They had not called an attorney, but one had shown up at their bail hearings anyway.

Felt said, "This thing has all kinds of political ramifications and the press is going to have a field day." That morning at 9 A.M., the *Post*'s city editor woke me at home with a phone call, asking me to cover an unusual burglary at the Watergate.

5

THE CALL THAT SUMMONED ME TO THE *POST* THAT Saturday morning was a classic example of what the newspaper does best—throw many reporters at a story, pile on, or as an executive editor for *The New York Times* would say decades later, "flood the zone." Eight reporters would work the Watergate story that first day, including Carl Bernstein. The editors were looking for anyone eager to join in. As a police reporter for the past nine months who was always looking for another assignment, I was available. The editors on the city desk immediately sent me to the local courthouse to cover the arraignment of the five burglars. Douglas Caddy, a well-dressed attorney, had shown up, saying he was not the attorney of record for the burglars but was simply watching the proceedings. He would say only that he had met one of the burglars at a social event. Right off the bat it seemed very strange.

The five burglars filed into the courtroom. All were dressed in business suits, less belts and neckties. They seated themselves in the same row, nervous, working their hands, stony silent.

U.S Attorney Earl Silbert was on hand personally to argue that the five should not be released on bail. Silbert, a Harvard Law School graduate, known as "Earl the Pearl" because of his dramatic, polished courtroom presentations and flowery language, noted the five had given false names, were not cooperating with the police, "possessed $2,300 in cold cash, and had a tendency to travel abroad." The burglary was "professional," with obvious "clandestine" intent, Silbert said.

Judge James A. Belsen asked the five arrayed before him what they did for a living. "Anti-communists," one declared, and the others nodded in agreement. The judge asked the tallest and oldest, the presumed leader, to step forward. James McCord, balding and deadpan serious, moved before the judge.

Occupation, the judge inquired.

"Security consultant," McCord answered.

Where?

In a low voice, McCord said that he was recently retired from government service. He was sending a strong message that he wanted this to be between the judge and him. It was an open courtroom so I moved to the front row and leaned as far into the conversation as possible without joining it.

"Where in government?" the judge inquired.

"CIA," McCord whispered, barely audible.

The judge flinched. Holy shit, I said half aloud. It was like a 10,000-volt jolt of electricity. I was amazed.

The first paragraph of the front page story that ran the next day in the *Post* read: "Five men, one of whom said he is a former employee of the Central Intelligence Agency, were arrested at 2:30 A.M. yesterday in what authorities described as an elaborate plot to bug the offices of the Democratic National Committee here."

The story carefully noted that, "There was no immediate explanation as to why the five suspects would want to bug the Democratic National Committee offices, or whether or not they were working for any other individuals or organizations." I could not know that this echoed Felt's own query, "What in the world were they doing?"

At that point, the president was ahead 19 points in the polls, and conventional wisdom held that Nixon was too smart to be party to any such bugging fiasco. He played ultimate political hardball, was crafty and tricky, but there was no compelling evidence that he was a serial lawbreaker.

The next day, Sunday, Carl and I were the only two who came to the office to follow up on the burglary. Both of us were divorced, no wives or children. A story moving on the Associated Press wire said that Nixon campaign expenditure records showed that McCord was the salaried security coordinator for CREEP. Working the phones, we were able to put together a portrait of McCord as the ultimate straight arrow—religious, a family man, a lieutenant colonel in the Air Force Reserve, a rocklike career government man, someone who followed orders. Carl and I wrote our first story together, identifying McCord as the salaried security coordinator for CREEP. The story was played on the front page in the upper left-hand corner.

After midnight, Eugene Bachinski, the *Post*'s best police reporter, called to tell me that he had learned that the address books of two of the burglars contained the phone number of an E. Howard Hunt Jr. with small notations "W. House" and "W.H." by his name.

On Monday I went to work on Hunt, furiously making calls to other numbers Bachinski supplied from the burglars' address books. It was not at all clear what I had, though the tantalizing "W. House" and "W.H." obviously meant the White House.

This was the sort of moment when a source or friend in the investigative agencies of government is invaluable. I called Felt at the FBI, reaching him through his secretary. It would be our first talk about Watergate. He reminded me how he disliked phone calls at the office but said that the burglary case was going to "heat up" for reasons he could not explain. He hung up abruptly.

I was tentatively assigned on the news budget to write the next day's Watergate bugging story, but I was still not sure that I had anything. Carl had the day off. I picked up the phone and dialed 456-1414—the White House—and asked for Howard Hunt. There was no answer but the operator said helpfully he might be in the office of Charles Colson, Nixon's special counsel. Colson's secretary said Hunt was not there but might be at a public relations firm where he worked as a writer. I called the firm, reached Hunt, and asked why his name was in the address books of two of the Watergate burglars.

"Good God!" Hunt shouted, said he had no comment and slammed down the phone. Later we learned he had immediately left town and gone into hiding. There was a certain I-am-packing-my-bags quality to the "Good God" that added to the mounting number of extraordinary curiosities.

I called the president of the public relations firm, Robert F. Bennett, who is now a U.S. senator from Utah. "I guess it's no secret that Howard was with the CIA," Bennett said blandly.

There it was again—CIA. It had been a secret to me, but a CIA spokesman openly confirmed that Hunt had been with the agency from 1949 to 1970.

I called Felt again at the FBI. Colson, White House, CIA,

I said. What do I have? Anyone could have someone's name in an address book. I wanted to be careful about guilt by association.

Felt sounded nervous. He said off the record—meaning I could not use the information—that Hunt was a prime suspect in the Watergate burglary for many reasons beyond the address books. So reporting the connections forcefully would not be unfair. Unknown to me at the time, the FBI had reviewed Hunt's White House personnel file and found that he had worked nearly 600 hours for Colson in less than a year.

Felt's assurance—knowing there was more there—was a critical and substantial buttress to the story. Eugene Bachinski and I wrote a front page article in the *Post* headlined, "White House Consultant Linked to Bugging Suspects." White House press secretary Ronald L. Ziegler said that "Certain elements may try to stretch this beyond what it is," but that Watergate was "a third-rate burglary," meriting no further White House comment.

It would be more than two years before it was learned, from the smoking-gun tapes which forced Nixon's resignation, that two days later, on June 23, 1972, the president ordered the CIA to attempt to get the FBI to halt and limit the Watergate inquiry on vague but insistent national security grounds.

At the time I had no idea of the degree to which Felt

sensed he was in jeopardy, or the momentum of the cover-up he was resisting. On Saturday, June 24, 1972—just a week after the break-in—Gray called in the special agent in charge of the Washington field office and 26 agents working the Watergate investigation, and accused them of suffering from "flapjaw." All were offended, as Gray would not permit them to defend themselves. "I literally put my track shoes in their backs," Gray reported later.

"The leaks continued, however," Felt wrote in his book, "and the *Washington Post*'s Woodward and Bernstein team was soon giving their readers details of the investigation, sometimes within hours after the Bureau learned of them. The White House was furious, and Ehrlichman called Gray on the carpet and told him, in no uncertain terms, that the leaks must stop." An inspection team—the goons—was sent to question all the agents, and then an assistant director grilled them under oath.

What I did not know at the time, but learned much later, was that John Dean called Felt and complained about leaks, demanding new steps to silence leakers. Felt refused. He was playing a dangerous game, and it would only get more dangerous.

By early July the delayed FBI interviews, and various impediments and obstructions, had reached a boiling point. At Nixon's instructions, the CIA was attempting to call off the FBI from tracing some $89,000 in Mexican checks

59

drawn by an attorney named Manuel Ogarrio. The checks had been deposited in the Miami bank account of one of the Watergate burglars, Bernard Barker.

On July 5, Felt made an appointment with Gray to protest, according to the account in Felt's book.

"Look," Felt told the acting director, "the reputation of the FBI is at stake. . . . We can't delay the Ogarrio interview any longer! I hate to make this sound like an ultimatum, but unless we get a request in writing from [CIA Director Richard] Helms to forgo the Ogarrio interview, we're going ahead anyway!"

It was stunning, near mutiny. Felt would never have spoken like that to Hoover. Gray bowed to the ultimatum, but Felt had already gone ahead and ordered the interview on his own. When Gray wondered if the investigation could not be confined to the five burglars, plus Hunt and Liddy, Felt said, "I am convinced we will be going much higher than these seven. These men are the pawns. We want the ones who moved the pawns!"

Later in July, Carl went to Miami, home of the four other burglars, on the money trail. He ingeniously tracked down a local prosecutor and his chief investigator, who had copies of the $89,000 in Mexican checks drawn by Ogarrio and another $25,000 check which had gone into Barker's account. We were able to establish that the $25,000 check had been campaign money that had been given to Maurice

H. Stans, Nixon's former commerce secretary and now the president's chief fund-raiser, on a Florida golf course. An August 1 story was the first to tie Nixon campaign money directly to Watergate.

I tried to call Felt at the FBI, but he wouldn't take the call. I tried his home in Virginia and had no better luck. So I showed up at his home one night that summer out in the Virginia suburbs. It was a plain-vanilla, perfectly kept, everything-in-its-place suburban home. His foreboding manner made me nervous and I thought he was ready to go through the roof. He seemed elated by the story connecting the burglars to Nixon campaign money, but Felt also seemed like a man who dreaded my presence. No more phones, he said, no more visits to his house, no more nothing out in the open.

Watergate was one hell of a story, I was sure. My confidence in that was reinforced by Felt's obvious consternation. I knew nothing about the obstruction and delaying tactics of the White House and Acting Director Gray, but obviously something was up.

I did not know then that in his earliest days in the FBI, Felt had been assigned to work on the general desk of the espionage section of the FBI. During World War II, he learned a great deal about German spying. As Felt would later recount in his book, *The FBI Pyramid*, a senior major case agent had passed on as routine a four-volume file involving a Nazi sympathizer named Maximilian G. W. Oth-mer. Felt had studied the file. Included was a letter from a Trenton dentist offhandedly noting that Othmer had begged him for a prescription for the painkiller Pyramidon. Felt knew that Pyramidon was used by Abwehr agents to make secret ink. He recommended a full investigation. Othmer soon confessed that he was sending secret-ink messages to a letter drop in Milan—R. A. Hombury, 46 Via Gran Sassa. A file search found two other suspected spies using the same mail drop. Later it was established that Othmer was a key Abwehr spy, supplying details on naval convoys and U.S. Navy readiness. He revealed a secret codebook for writing a message in routine plain text. "Mrs." meant a convoy; if the name began with A it meant a convoy of under 10 ships; if a B, 10 to 20 ships; if C, 20 to 30. Suitcase meant a destroyer, etc.

Felt was promoted to the major case desk, where he worked on concealed messages in microdots and a double-agent operation code-named "Peasant" to supply false data to the enemy military. After the war, he was assigned to work against the Soviet espionage apparatus, and he spent time on the street in espionage surveillance. Surveillance of Nicolai Reddin, a Russian naval officer stationed in Seattle, was difficult because Reddin knew all the tricks—making prohibited left turns, backtracking, being patient as he moved to meetings, concealment.

So at his home in Virginia in the summer of 1972, Felt said that if we were to talk it would have to be face-to-face where no one could observe us.

Anything would be fine with me, I said.

We would need a preplanned notification system—a change in the environment that no one else would notice or attach any meaning to, he said.

I didn't know what he was talking about.

If you keep the drapes in your apartment closed, open them and that could signal me, he said. He could check each day or have them checked, and if they were open we could meet that night at a predesignated place.

I like to let the light in at times, I explained.

We need another signal, he said, indicating that he could check my apartment regularly. He never explained how he could do this.

Feeling under some pressure, I said that I had a red cloth flag, less than a foot square—the kind used on long truck-loads—that a girlfriend had found on the street. She had stuck it in an empty flowerpot on my apartment balcony.

Felt and I quickly agreed that I would move the flowerpot with the flag, which normally was in the front near the railing, to the rear of the balcony if I needed an urgent meeting. This would have to be important and rare, he said sternly. The signal, he said, would mean we would meet that same night about 2 A.M. on the bottom level of an underground garage just over Key Bridge in Rosslyn, Virginia. The garage was behind and underneath 1401 Wilson Boulevard—a large, tall building. The garage entrance that I used is now 1820 North Nash Street. Rosslyn, a built-up area of office buildings and hotels on the Virginia side of the Potomac River, is just north of Arlington Cemetery and the Pentagon.

Okay, I said.

Felt said that I would have to observe strict counter-surveillance techniques.

Which were? I asked.

How did I get out of my apartment?

I walked out, down the hall and took the elevator.

Which takes you to the lobby? he asked.

Yes.

Did I have back stairs to my apartment house?

Yes.

Use them when you are heading for a meeting. Do they open into an alley?

Yes.

Take the alley. Don't use your own car. Take a taxicab to a point several blocks from a hotel where there are cabs after midnight. Get dropped off and then walk to get a second cab to Rosslyn. Don't get dropped off directly at the parking garage. Walk the last several blocks. If you are being followed, don't go down to the garage. I'll understand if you don't show.

All this was like a lecture. The key was taking the necessary time—an hour or two to get there. Be patient, serene. Trust the prearrangements. There was no fallback meeting place or time. If one of us didn't show, there would be no meeting, he said.

Felt said that if he had something for me, he could get me a message. He quizzed me about my daily routine, what came to my apartment, the mailbox, etc. The *Post* was delivered outside my apartment door. I had a subscription to *The New York Times*, as did a number of people in my apartment building. The copies were left in the lobby with the apartment number. Mine was No. 617 and it was written clearly on the outside of each paper in marker pen.

Felt said if there was something important he could get to my *New York Times*. I never knew how. Page 20 would be circled and hands of a clock in the lower part of the page would be drawn to indicate the time of the meeting that night, probably 2 A.M., in the same Rosslyn parking garage. The relationship with him was a compact of trust; nothing about it was to be discussed or shared with anyone, he said.

I had never heard of such extreme precautions. It was extraordinary. His help on the Wallace assassination attempt gave me a real pipeline into the FBI. I was more than willing to comply with his request. The details of what was obviously spy tradecraft, Felt's experience or common sense were appealing. He was taking this as seriously, or more seriously, than I was. In technical journalistic terms, the information he might supply was on "deep background." This meant the information could be used if it were thought reliable or could be confirmed, but no source would be cited—not an FBI, Justice Department or administration source. That way a specific comment or piece of information could not be traced back to him. He said he was not going to be giving me specific information from the FBI investigation or FBI files. The trick was to use him as a backstop or second source for information and conclusions gathered elsewhere. He could steer me toward what was right, or toward a fruitful line of inquiry. Clearly, Felt wanted the greatest detachment—full deniability—from the stories Carl and I were writing.

How he might have made a daily observation of my balcony is still a mystery to me. At the time, before the era of intensive security, the back of my apartment building at 1718 P Street Northwest, which was called the Webster House, was not enclosed with a wall or a fence, as it is today. Anyone could have driven in the back alley to observe my balcony. In addition, my balcony and the back of the apartment complex faced onto a courtyard or back area that was shared with a number of other apartment or office buildings in the area. My balcony could have been seen from dozens of apartments or offices.

There were a number of foreign embassies in the area.

The Iraqi embassy was down the street at 18th and P Streets, and I thought it possible that the FBI had surveillance or listening posts in the area. Could Felt have had the counterintelligence agents regularly report on the status of my flag and flowerpot? That seems highly unlikely but not impossible. How he did it or whether he intended to check or did in fact check each day is unknown to me. He did miss several meetings I later requested.

In the course of this and other conversations, I was somewhat apologetic for plaguing him, for being such a nag, but we had nowhere else to turn. Carl and I had obtained a list of everyone who worked for Nixon's reelection committee and were frequently going out into the night knocking on the doors of these people to try to interview them. I explained to Felt that we were getting lots of doors slammed in our faces. There also were lots of frightened looks. Nixon people were certainly intimidated by reporters. I was frustrated.

Felt said that I shouldn't worry about pushing him. He had done his time as a street agent, interviewing people. The FBI, like the press, had to rely on people's voluntary cooperation. Most wanted to help the FBI, but the FBI knew about rejection. Howard Hunt, for one, had told the FBI that he had hired a lawyer who had advised him to have nothing whatsoever to do with law enforcement agencies. Hunt would not even tell the FBI the name of his attorney, Felt said.

The payoff for pushing hard was evident in his own career, he told me once. Getting the meeting with Hoover had clearly made a difference. Eventually he became the assistant special agent in charge of the New Orleans field office, and later was promoted to become SAC in Salt Lake City, a region that included Mafia-infested Las Vegas.

Felt's message to me was unusual, emphatically encouraging me to get in his face.

Only later would I learn from FBI files that on September 1, 1972, U.S. Attorney Earl Silbert, the chief Watergate prosecutor, asked the FBI to "electronically sweep his office as well as the federal grand jury area" because of stories appearing in *The Washington Post* that included information given to the grand jury. Felt's "F" appears at the time, indicating he had seen the memo. The sweep was conducted September 5 and no wiretaps or room bugs were discovered.

6

ON SEPTEMBER 15, A FEDERAL GRAND JURY indicted Hunt, Liddy and the five Watergate burglars. No higher-ups were charged or mentioned. It was depressing. We hoped that Silbert had come up with something new. Carl and I were onto the secret cash fund kept by the Nixon reelection committee. We were sure it had financed the Watergate operation and that assistants to former Attorney General John Mitchell had controlled the money. The day after the indictment I broke the rule about telephone contact with Felt and called him. Carl and I had drafted a story about how high officials at the Nixon campaign had been involved in the funding of the Watergate burglary.

"Too soft," he said to my astonishment. "You can go

much stronger." He prodded me with veiled and thin references to "other intelligence-gathering activities" beyond Watergate. He said that Mitchell's top assistants were among those who controlled a fund which we had determined from CREEP treasurer Hugh Sloan had $300,000 for such operations. Carl and I wrote a story that was thin on details, but that suggested the Watergate indictments had not broken the conspiracy.

Carl had tracked down the bookkeeper to the Nixon campaign, Judy Hoback, and she eventually opened up about many cash withdrawals from this secret cash fund. The bookkeeper had finally said that three people—Gordon Liddy and two of the campaign's senior officials, deputy campaign manager Jeb Stuart Magruder and campaign aide Bart Porter—had all received in excess of $50,000 in cash from the secret fund. That was a story, but it needed confirmation and context.

I again broke the no-telephone rule, calling Felt at home on a Sunday afternoon. I was desperate but I knew that he admired persistence, even though he had told me not to call. I was trying to play by the larger principle—persistence at all costs. When he heard my voice, there was a long pause. This would have to be our last telephone conversation, he said angrily. He confirmed the cash payments to Magruder and Porter, indicating that the money flow was important. This later was reduced to the slogan "Follow the money," a phrase which as best I can recall he never used. For decades I had thought he used that precise phrase, but it is not in our book, *All the President's Men,* and I cannot find it in any of my notes. But that certainly was the idea.

Twenty years after the break-in, when I reviewed the Watergate files at the FBI, I found on page 3 of a 10-page summary of an FBI interview with Hoback on July 18 that she had said there were notations of such disbursements to Porter and Magruder. But in the conversation that day, Felt sounded worried and disgusted—guarded, serious, even haunted. Some of his humor returned when he finally said, "Let's just say I'll be willing to put the blossoming situation in perspective for you when the time comes." He repeated that he didn't want any more phone calls from me. The phone calls obviously troubled him. But clearly there was an upside to all this, he indicated. Things were about to come crashing down.

To demonstrate his ambivalence about everything, even the phone calls, Felt said in apparent contradiction that if I absolutely had to call, I should not identify myself but just say something or ask for someone else. He would recognize my voice, and then we would meet that night in the parking garage.

I reached Magruder that Sunday afternoon before the story ran the next day. Magruder was second in command at the Nixon reelection committee and formerly he had been the deputy communications director at the White House. He flatly denied receiving $50,000 in cash, said he had been questioned about it "and it was agreed by all parties that it is incorrect." But his voice shook as we talked.

Later in September, Carl and I interviewed Hugh Sloan, the Nixon campaign treasurer who had resigned in disgust after Watergate. We reported that the secret fund and disbursements had been controlled by Mitchell, among others. Carl reached Mitchell by phone and the former attorney general said, "Katie Graham's gonna get her tit caught in a big fat wringer if that's published." It was published as we sharpened our focus on the money trail.

But money for what other than Watergate?

Because of the stories Carl and I were doing, Sandy Ungar, the Post's regular Justice Department reporter, had suggested that I interview someone by the name of W. Mark Felt, the associate FBI director, to see if he would help me. As I recall, Ungar said that I should call Felt at the FBI, suggesting that he was anticipating my call.

I was in a tizzy. What was going on? Was this a setup of some kind? Given the alternatives, I figured it was best to call Felt's office. I arranged an interview through his secretary, I believe. I didn't know what to do, but I decided that it was best to show up.

When I arrived at Felt's office he was sitting behind his

desk. His assistant was present as a kind of hall monitor. A most uncomfortable charade proceeded. I said I wanted confirmation on some matters that Carl and I had discovered. I don't even remember what they were. Felt was proper. He wouldn't answer anything. I don't think he was rolling his eyes, but mine were spinning. Even in the most useless interview with the most tight-lipped person, a reporter can generally get something, even if it's a negative. Never has so little been said. I can't even find if I took notes. Felt and I never discussed the meeting, but he mentioned it in his 1979 book as evidence that he had never helped me.

IN LATE SEPTEMBER 1972, a late-night caller told Carl that a friend named Alex Shipley, an assistant attorney general for the state of Tennessee, had been asked to work to disrupt, sabotage and spy on Democratic presidential candidates. Carl called Shipley, who confirmed the story. Carl eventually found three attorneys who had been asked to conduct such activities by an attorney named Donald H. Segretti.

It was bizarre. Somehow Segretti had been interviewed by the FBI as part of the Watergate investigation, but it was not clear what the relationship might be, or how serious it was. Carl wanted to write a story about Segretti's efforts to recruit people for dirty tricks.

I was in New York City for the weekend and a draft of a story was read to me over the phone. Not enough details, I argued. What was their scope or purpose? I promised to come back to Washington and contact "my friend," the code I used for Mark Felt. The memos I typed from our interviews had "X" at the top, or in one case, "M.F." It stood for my friend, but of course they were Mark Felt's initials, hardly first-rate tradecraft to protect his identity.

I caught the late Eastern shuttle back to Washington. It was many years later that I learned that Felt had had a particularly bad week as the White House efforts to stall, thwart and obstruct the investigation continued. John Dean himself, or another White House or Nixon reelection committee lawyer, was sitting in on the FBI interviews, chilling low and midlevel people from providing information candidly. For Felt, the worst was Gray's acquiescence to Dean's request for copies of the raw 302 form interview reports and Teletypes about the FBI investigation. That week, on October 2, 1972, Gray had turned over dozens of such reports to Dean—an unheard-of sharing of investigative files with a potential target of the inquiry.

When my plane landed, I called Felt at home. I did not identify myself but mumbled something vague. He seemed to recognize my voice.

Okay, he said, or something like that.

I took that to mean we could meet that night in the

garage. With time to kill, I got some food at the airport, probably read some and took a cab to a hotel, waited 10 or more minutes and got a second cab to Rosslyn. I was simultaneously put off and thrilled by the clandestine nature of the meeting. It was unprecedented for me. It also was quite scary that late at night. I found the building and went down to the bottom floor of the underground garage.

Felt was there waiting. He had lit a cigarette. I never knew if he was a regular smoker or whether it was the nervousness of these moments. Later he claimed that he had given up smoking in 1943, but I have known many who say they quit but take a lone cigarette in times of immense stress. Normally, he was quite debonair with his well-combed mop of gray hair and a sly, pleasant, kind of all-knowing, even smug smile. That night he seemed thinner and I could see in the light that his eyes were bloodshot.

He seemed glad to see me. After all, we were the only two in this underground-garage foxhole. He probably welcomed the company. It was a frightening, lonely place with few if any parked cars on our level of the garage. Felt probably was carrying his gun, but I didn't even own one.

"There is a way to untie the Watergate knot," he said. "I can't and won't give you any new names, but everything points in the direction of what was called 'Offensive Security.'"

I thought this term, "Offensive Security," which I had never heard before, was important, but to my knowledge it was never used again, never resurfaced in the many Watergate investigations. Decades later, reviewing everything Felt said to me, it is apparent he was wrong on a number of things.

"Remember, you don't do those 1,500 interviews and not have something on your hands other than a single break-in," he said, referring to the number of interviews the FBI had conducted in the Watergate investigation so far—a point that had been advertised by the White House as evidence that the Watergate investigation had been thorough.

"Mitchell was involved," Felt said. There was no doubt about it. John Ehrlichman, Nixon's chief domestic policy adviser, had ordered Howard Hunt to leave town, he said.

That struck me as hard to believe. Ehrlichman's fingerprints had not yet appeared in Watergate or other operations.

The scope of the illegal activities and dirty tricks was large, Felt said, adding that we should check every lead. "You could write stories from now until Christmas or well beyond that."

I asked about Segretti.

Felt wouldn't answer specifically. But everything was tied in. "Just remember what I'm saying. Everything was part of it. . . . I know what I'm talking about."

He continued on Mitchell. "That guy definitely learned some things in those ten days after Watergate." If it all came out it could ruin the administration, Felt said. Mitchell realized that he was personally ruined.

It would not be until the next year, in testimony before the Senate Watergate Committee, that Mitchell would say he learned about what he called the "White House horrors"—additional illegal operations.

Felt emphasized the depth of the operation. He said he knew of dirty tricks in Illinois, New York, New Hampshire, Massachusetts, California, Texas, Florida and D.C.

What about Howard Hunt's efforts to plug leaks?

"That operation was not only to check leaks to the papers but often to manufacture items for the press," he said. It would be some time before it was revealed that Hunt had tried to alter classified cables to indicate falsely that President Kennedy was responsible for the 1963 assassination of South Vietnamese President Ngo Dinh Diem.

We talked for so long that eventually Felt and I sat down on the dirty garage floor. Was the White House behind all this? I asked, pressing for specifics once again.

"Of course, of course, don't you get my message?" He was exasperated and stood up. Then he clammed up suddenly. I finally grabbed his arm and said we were playing a degrading chickenshit game pretending that he was not passing original, new information to me. Of course, he was.

"Okay," he said. "This is very serious." Segretti was not a lone operator. "You can safely say that 50 people worked for the White House and CREEP to play games and spy and sabotage and gather intelligence. Some of it is beyond belief, kicking at the opposition in every imaginable way. You already know some of it."

He nodded confirmation as I recited a list that Carl and I had gathered from others about the tactics used by the White House and the reelection campaign—bugging, following people, false press leaks, fake letters, canceling campaign rallies, investigating campaign workers' private lives, planting spies, stealing documents, planting provocateurs in political demonstrations.

Then Felt crossed a significant line, uttering the unthinkable: "It's all in the files." Heretofore the files had been sacred, unmentionable. "Justice and the Bureau know about it, even though it wasn't followed up." The Watergate investigation had been confined to the June 17 break-in and bugging operation.

And there were more or less 50 saboteurs or spies out there like Segretti?

"You can safely say more than 50," Felt repeated. He looked more than tired, even queasy. It was nearly 6 A.M.

I went home and slept for several hours and then went to the *Post*. Since I had not taken notes, I typed a three-page memo to share with Carl and the editors.

Three decades later, as I review the original of that memo, I see that Felt mentioned several matters that Carl and I did not use in the *Post* or in *All the President's Men* because they might have made it clear that Deep Throat was in the FBI. Felt had said that night in the garage that all the FBI reports that showed the widespread nature of Watergate and associated activities were never put together *"except on Gray's desk—and that we don't like."* In addition, he said, someone in the government wanted to sue the *Post* to get at our sources. He also referred to the ITT scandal. At the end of the meeting, Felt said, *"don't quote any of that 'not one word' in the paper . . . this is just for your background."* The last line of the memo makes it clear that he had access to documents in the investigation. It reads: *"no documents 'I'd never do that on this case.'"*

Now we had perhaps our most important story. Carl typed out the lead:

"FBI agents have established that the Watergate bugging incident stemmed from a massive campaign of political spying and sabotage conducted on behalf of President Nixon's re-election and directly by officials of the White House and Committee for the Re-election of the President.

"The activities, according to information in FBI and Department of Justice files, were aimed at all the major Democratic presidential contenders and—since 1971— represented a basic strategy of the Nixon re-election effort."

It was very aggressive, interpretive language. I knew that Felt would object to the declaration that it was in FBI files. So much was from him. Segretti was not mentioned until the 18th paragraph and the detail "50 undercover Nixon operatives" was in the 19th paragraph.

The story ran as the lead story on October 10, 1972, under a four-column, two-line headline on the top half of page 1: "FBI Finds Nixon Aides/Sabotaged Democrats." The comment from the Nixon campaign was simple. It was included in the third paragraph: "The *Post* story is not only fiction but a collection of absurdities."

At the Washington bureau of *The New York Times* they were scrambling when our first edition came out at about 11 P.M. Within several hours, *Times* reporters had contacted the three attorneys whom Segretti had attempted to recruit. The *Times*'s story at the bottom of page 1 in its late editions summarized the *Post*'s allegations of a nationwide Nixon-run and Nixon-financed espionage and sabotage campaign.

Election day was less than a month away. At the White House, press secretary Ron Ziegler declined 29 times in the course of a half-hour briefing to answer questions about our story.

What is rather astonishing is that the FBI to my knowledge made no public comment. The story clearly pinned the conclusion on the FBI, stating in the headline that the

"FBI Finds . . ." and in the story that the FBI had "established. . . ."

FBI files that I have since reviewed show that during the summer of 1972 the Bureau had interviewed Segretti and others (including top White House aides) involved in his activities. The FBI approach was to conclude that Segretti's activities were basically political "harassment."

Two days after our story, D. J. Dalbey, an FBI headquarters official, sent Felt a three-page memo saying, "We should not be surprised to learn that Segretti has violated several federal laws, but the known facts are too few to permit a conclusion at this time." Felt had reached his conclusion, had apparently been unable get the investigation expanded, and he decided to talk to me instead.

The top Justice officials did not want an expanded investigation. One FBI memo dated March 21, 1973, says that U.S. Attorney Earl Silbert, who was running the Watergate investigation at that point, "was satisfied that the activities of these men (like Segretti) were political and that they were not involved in nor were they part of the Watergate conspiracy." Assistant Attorney General Henry E. Petersen, who was in charge of the Justice Department criminal division and had supervisory responsibility for Silbert and the Watergate investigation, agreed according to this and other memos.

Charles Bolz, the chief of the FBI's accounting and fraud

section, wrote in an October 18, 1972, memo—just eight days after the *Post*'s story—about the head of the criminal division: "Mr. Petersen advised he was fully aware of the extent of the FBI's investigation of Segretti and he is also aware of the allegations as to Segretti's political harassment activities and attempts to recruit personnel to assist in such, as set forth in recent news articles. Mr. Petersen stated he does not believe Segretti's activities are in violation of any federal statutes and, accordingly, he can see no basis for requesting any additional investigation of Segretti by the FBI at this time."

Segretti and many others later received jail sentences when the full nature of Watergate was investigated by a special prosecutor.

The weekend after the October 10 Segretti-espionage-sabotage story, Carl and I published stories based on information from sources other than Felt indicating that Segretti had been hired for the campaign sabotage by Dwight Chapin, President Nixon's appointments secretary. Chapin met almost daily with Nixon and was one of a handful of White House aides with easy access to the president.

The second story said that Herbert Kalmbach, Nixon's personal attorney, had paid Segretti some $35,000 of campaign money to finance his spying and sabotage campaign.

Watergate was closing in on the White House and the president himself. It turns out that much of the information about Chapin as Segretti's contact and Kalmbach as his bankroller had been obtained months earlier by the FBI and the Watergate grand jury that was being run by U.S. Attorney Silbert. That the criminal investigation was not expanded aggressively to these matters shows how effective the Nixon White House and Justice Department had been in diverting and covering up.

After those weekend stories, the White House and Nixon campaign let loose on the *Post*. Bob Dole, the Republican national chairman, delivered a speech in which he devoted three pages to connecting our reporting with the campaign of Nixon's opponent, Senator George McGovern, the Democratic nominee for president. Dole (who many years later apologized to me) said that the *Post* was McGovern's "partner in mud slinging. . . . Mr. McGovern appears to have turned over the franchise for his media attack campaign to the editors of *The Washington Post,* who have shown themselves every bit as sure-footed along the low road of this campaign as their candidate."

Clark MacGregor, successor to Mitchell as the head of the Nixon campaign, scheduled a special news conference to attack the *Post*.

"Using innuendo, third-person hearsay, unsubstantiated charges, anonymous sources and huge scare headlines, the *Post* has maliciously sought to give the appearance of a direct connection between the White House and Watergate—

a charge the *Post* knows and half a dozen investigations have found to be false."

We were on solid ground. But like many who are on a roll, we would overreach. Hugh Sloan, the ex-CREEP campaign treasurer, had told us that a top White House aide was one of the people who controlled the secret cash fund of hundreds of thousands of dollars that had been used to finance Watergate, other political spying and sabotage. Carl and I figured it had to be H. R. "Bob" Haldeman, 46, Nixon's White House chief of staff, the buttoned-down, crew-cut former ad man who ran things for the president. But Sloan wouldn't answer any Haldeman questions.

7

ON OCTOBER 19, I MOVED THE FLOWERPOT BACK, hoping to set a meeting that night in Rosslyn.

That same afternoon, as we would learn years later, Nixon met in his hideaway office in the Executive Office Building with Haldeman. The secret taping system captured their discussion.

Haldeman reported that he had learned authoritatively from his own secret source, which he would not name for the president, that there was a leak in the FBI.

"Somebody next to Gray?" Nixon inquired.

"Mark Felt," Haldeman said.

"Now why the hell would he do that?" the president asked.

"You can't say anything about this, because it will screw

up our source and there's a real concern. Mitchell is the only one that knows this and he feels very strongly that we better not do anything because—"

"Do anything?" Nixon interrupted, adding incredulously, "Never?"

"If we move on him," Haldeman warned, "he'll go out and unload everything. He knows everything that's to be known in the FBI. He has access to absolutely everything."

Haldeman reported that he had asked John Dean what to do about Felt. "He says you can't prosecute him, that he hasn't committed a crime. . . . Dean's concerned if you let him know now he'll go out and go on network television."

"You know what I'd do with him, the bastard," Nixon said. "Well, that's all I want to hear about it."

Haldeman said that Felt wanted the top spot at the FBI.

"Is he Catholic?" the president asked.

"No, sir. He's Jewish."

"Christ, put a Jew in there?" Nixon replied.

"Well, that could explain it too," Haldeman said.

Later Nixon asked, "What's the conveyor belt for Felt?"

"The *Post*," Haldeman answered.

Nixon pressed for the White House's source, and Haldeman said the information came to them from some "legal guy," presumably someone who worked at the *Post*. "He knows that the FBI is leaking to a reporter in his publication," Haldeman said.

"So say nothing . . ." Nixon ordered.

This meant that we at the *Post* perhaps had our own Deep Throat problem, someone who was leaking information to the Justice Department and the White House about our sources. We never found out who might have been providing information from the *Post*, but the White House apparently came very close to establishing that one of our sources was Felt.

That evening, October 19, I took all the precautions—two cabs, watchfulness, patience. When I arrived, it was 2:30 A.M. I was late but Felt was not there. I waited an hour. In the underlit cold garage I had some paranoid thoughts. Surely those mad enough to hire Gordon Liddy and Howard Hunt might do something unthinkable. It was hard to assess the level of danger if indeed there was any. Surely Haldeman could learn that Carl and I were making inquiries. Had Felt been spotted? Had I been followed? It seemed irrational on my part, so I walked outside to look around. Steeling myself, I finally walked back down into the black. I looked around, spent some time stewing in my fear, calmed myself and finally left. I was terrified. I ran out and raced home.

I told Carl that Deep Throat had not shown up. We were worried. The following day, my *New York Times* had page 20 circled and the time indicated 3 A.M. I arrived early. Felt was already there. He said he had not been able to check the balcony but that everything about Watergate was heating up even more. He didn't have to tell me.

Though Carl and I did not in fact have it, I told Felt that we were going to publish a story the next week saying that Haldeman was the final and fifth person to control the secret fund.

"You've got to do it on your own," Felt said.

I said that I expected him to warn me if we were wrong. Felt said he would.

So he was essentially confirming Haldeman?

"I'm not," he said. "You've got to do it on your own."

It was a distinction that didn't make sense to me. I was tired of this dancing around.

"You cannot use me as a source," Felt said. "I won't be a source on a Haldeman story." He warned me to be careful. But he said he would try to keep us out of trouble.

Are we in trouble on Haldeman? I asked.

"I'll keep you out," Felt said ambiguously.

Well, I said, that meant he was confirming the Haldeman story.

Shifting direction once again, he said ominously that if I expected him to warn me off an inaccurate story that "*would be a misconception of our friendship.*"

On that terrible note, we shook hands and he left. I was persuaded that Haldeman was the correct name, but I was also convinced that Haldeman had frightening power.

Monday, October 23, I went over all this with Carl, who was uncomfortable. Did we have a confirmation?

Yes and no, I said. We both knew that in practical newspaper terms that meant no.

We went again to see Hugh Sloan, the treasurer who had kept the secret fund. Sloan, who had earlier worked in the Nixon White House for Haldeman, was also cagey about his former boss. Carl asked him if there would be anything wrong if we wrote that Haldeman was the fifth person.

"Let me put it this way, then," Sloan said. "I have no problems if you write a story like that." Sloan also said that he had told everything to the Watergate grand jury— answered all the questions accurately and fully.

After some memorable contortions with other sources, who seemed to confirm the story, we went with it. This was a different story. It named Haldeman as the fifth person to control the secret fund that had financed Watergate and other campaign spying and sabotage. We attributed it to Sloan's grand jury testimony. That would give it a solid basis. No more citing unidentified sources. The headline to the *Post*'s lead story October 25, 1972: "Testimony Ties Top Nixon Aide to Secret Fund." After all, Sloan had not only told us explicitly that it was Haldeman, he pledged that he had answered all the grand jury questions.

This was a case where one plus one didn't add up to two, as we would soon find out. The next day Sloan's attorney,

James Stoner, said before the television cameras, "Our answer to that is an unequivocal no. We did not—Mr. Sloan did not implicate Mr. Haldeman in that testimony at all."

All hell broke loose. Carl and I thought we might have to resign from the *Post*. Sloan finally told us that yes, indeed, Haldeman had controlled the fund, but Sloan had never been asked about that by the grand jury. So, of course, he had not testified about it. It was a near disaster.

At the White House, as the tapes would later show, Nixon had been planning to challenge the television licenses owned by the Washington Post Company. At 12:29 P.M. on the day the Haldeman story ran, Nixon met with Charles Colson.

Of the *Post*, the president said, "We're going to screw them another way. They don't really realize how rough I can play. . . . But when I start, I will kill them. There's no question about it."

THE NEXT MORNING I moved the flag and flowerpot back on my balcony. When I got home about 9 P.M., I made myself an Ovaltine milkshake, my then-favorite comfort food. I fell asleep and almost missed the meeting in Rosslyn.

Felt was waiting.

For some 15 minutes I spilled out all my feelings of confusion and regret, pleading for help.

"Well," Felt said, "Haldeman slipped away from you."

Felt stomped his heel into the garage wall. The truth would never come out now, the error about Haldeman had sealed it, he said. He said that moving on the top man meant you had to be on the most solid ground. Felt cursed. He moved closer and whispered. "From top to bottom, this whole business is a Haldeman operation. He ran the money. Insulated himself through those functionaries around him."

He described Haldeman's chief aides in some detail. "Everybody goes chicken after you make a mistake like you guys made." I felt chastised. The story, Felt continued, was "the worst possible setback. You've got people feeling sorry for Haldeman. I didn't think that was possible."

He gave me a little lecture about breaking a conspiracy like Watergate. "You build convincingly from the outer edges in, you get ten times the evidence you need against the Hunts and Liddys. They feel hopelessly finished—they may not talk right away, but the grip is on them. Then you move up and do the same thing at the next level. If you shoot too high and miss, then everybody feels more secure. Lawyers work this way. I'm sure smart reporters must too." I recall he gave me a look as if to say I did not belong in that category of smart reporters. "You put the investigation back months. It puts everyone on the defensive—editors, FBI agents, everybody has to go into a crouch after this."

Eventually, Carl and I attempted to untangle what had happened for the *Post* readers, and included in another story information that the *Post* story was "incorrect" in attributing the Haldeman story to Sloan's grand jury testimony. But then we cited sources saying that Haldeman indeed did control the secret fund. The sources were Sloan and Felt.

"One source went so far as to say 'this is a Haldeman operation,' and Haldeman had 'insulated' himself."

I had very bad feelings about quoting Felt so directly. It really was contrary to the rules we had established of deep background. But I was frantic to get a story in the paper correcting our mistake.

I didn't try to contact Felt for some time and did not see him in the underground garage until late January 1973, almost three months later. In that time, Nixon had won re-election and the first Watergate trial of the burglars, and Hunt and Liddy, had finished without anything coming out about any involvement of higher-ups. It was a dead end. Carl and I did write stories about the trial. One was a news analysis summary headlined, "Still Secret: Who Hired the Spies and Why." We had already answered the question in the *Post* and the trial hadn't added much. We still needed detail. John J. Sirica, the trial judge, was unhappy that all the evidence had not been brought forward and he had lots of questions, papering his courtroom with skepticism. Years later, the judge told me that he had read our stories in the *Post*. The failure of the prosecution's case at trial to square with what we were reporting had added to his consternation about the government's failure to get to the bottom of the scandal.

When I met with Felt on January 25, I said that Carl and I were working on a big story about Mitchell and Colson—the two keys to the operations. Felt didn't bring up the Haldeman story in which I had quoted the unnamed source, namely him, about it being a "Haldeman operation." I certainly did not bring it up.

"Colson and Mitchell were behind the Watergate operation," Felt said. "Everyone in the FBI is convinced, including Gray." Someone had to break and talk. "No firsthand account," as he called it, meaning no progress.

Carl and I had some serious differences about what we had, and whether we should do a story about Mitchell and Colson. The fact was, we had nothing new, as we soon both realized.

The only good news was that Senator Sam J. Ervin, the 76-year-old North Carolina Democrat, called me to his office and said he was going to head a full Senate investigation of Watergate. He wanted leads and sources. I couldn't name sources, but I told him there was a lot in the newspaper stories Carl and I had done.

Ervin was aware of the articles. "Now, I believe that everyone who has been mentioned in your and Mr. Bernstein's accounts should be given an opportunity to come down and exonerate himself," Ervin said. "And if they decline, we'll subpoena them to ensure they have a chance to clear their names." His large eyebrows danced, and he smiled broadly as he said this.

Even the CIA, even top White House aides, he said. "Mr. Haldeman or Mr. Whomever."

Carl and I wrote a story for the front page outlining Ervin's plan to investigate fully and to call Nixon's top aides.

But soon Carl and I were back tracing the activities of Hunt and Liddy. That led to the Dita Beard story about Howard Hunt's visit to her hospital room in Denver, Felt's internal cover-your-ass FBI memo seeking a leak investigation, and the unusual meeting with Felt in the Prince George's County bar.

The next month, March, Watergate exploded with McCord's letter to Judge Sirica alleging a high-level cover-up. In April, there were almost daily explosions, including testimony that Liddy had three meetings with Mitchell, Dean and Magruder to plan the intelligence gathering and Watergate operations.

On the evening of April 16, the *Post's* night city editor called me at home to say that the *Los Angeles Times* had a front page story for the next day saying that the White House would make a dramatic Watergate admission soon.

Felt had agreed that I could call him at home from a pre-designated phone booth in an emergency. If he answered, I would say nothing, wait precisely 10 seconds and then hang up. He would know who it was and call the phone booth, which was in the lobby of the Madison Hotel across from the *Post*. Again the tradecraft was weak. I had to wait an hour before he called back.

"You don't have to tell me why you called," Felt said.

What was going on? I inquired. Rumors were everywhere.

"You'd better hang on for this," he said. "Dean and Haldeman are out—for sure. Out. They'll resign. There's no way the president can avoid it." He said it was solid. "Several are talking—go find out," he said, sounding like an assignment editor. "I've got to go. I mean it—find out."

The next morning, April 17, Carl and I reported to Bradlee and the other editors what Deep Throat had said.

Bradlee was reluctant to go with such a story, even though Deep Throat had said it was solid. He recalled how dangerous it was to anticipate high-level resignations. Back during the Johnson presidency, he said, Bill Moyers, a top Johnson aide, had been a source for a story that Johnson was going to replace J. Edgar Hoover at the FBI. Bradlee, who was the Washington bureau chief for *Newsweek*, had done a cover story saying the search for Hoover's successor is finally underway. The day *Newsweek* appeared on the stands, Johnson called a press conference. Just before, Johnson told Bill Moyers, "You call up Ben Bradlee and tell him,

'Fuck you.'" Johnson then went out and announced that he had appointed Hoover the director for life. For years, Bradlee said, people blamed him for Hoover's lifetime appointment.

We held the story about Haldeman and Dean.

Around this time it was also announced that the *Post* was being awarded the public service Pulitzer Prize for its reporting on Watergate.

About 7:45 P.M. on April 26, someone on Capitol Hill called me to say that the New York *Daily News* was running a story saying that Acting FBI Director Gray had destroyed documents taken from Howard Hunt's White House safe in the days after the Watergate burglary. Two folders had been deep-sixed. One folder contained the phony State Department cables fabricated by Hunt to implicate President Kennedy in the 1963 assassination of South Vietnamese President Ngo Dinh Diem.

The second folder was a dossier collected by Hunt on Senator Edward Kennedy.

About 9:30 P.M. my phone at the *Post* rang.

"Give me a number to call you on," Mark Felt said.

I gave him a basic city desk line and picked it up myself when the call came in.

"You've heard the Gray story?" Felt said. "Well, it's true." In a meeting with John Ehrlichman and John Dean, Gray was told the files were political dynamite that could do more damage than the Watergate bugging. Gray had taken the folders to his home in Connecticut, kept them for nearly six months, and burned them with the Christmas trash in December 1972.

The significance of Gray, the acting director of the FBI, destroying potential evidence was immense. It meant Gray was finished. I could hear a certain joy in Felt's voice.

Carl and I wrote the story for the next day's paper. That day Gray resigned. Felt thought he would finally become director. One wire service so reported and Felt had his secretary spend a half-hour getting his biographical information and photos together. For nearly three hours Felt was acting director and he immediately gave orders abolishing the so-called accountability log that required signatures from anyone seeing a sensitive document or report. The log was designed to stop leaks and it was affixed to each document. It often took more sheets of paper than the document itself and the logs began to resemble political nominating petitions.

Felt did not get the job. Nixon named William D. Ruckelshaus, who had been head of the Environmental Protection Agency, as acting director. In his book years later Felt wrote how he labeled the day Ruckelshaus arrived at the Bureau "blue Monday." Felt and the other top FBI officials sent a telegram to Nixon urging him to pick someone from within the Bureau as permanent director. Felt wrote that he was in despair over conditions, disillusioned and "jarred by the sight of Ruckelshaus lolling in an easy chair with his feet on what I still felt was J. Edgar Hoover's desk."

When the White House wanted records and lists of people the FBI had wiretapped during previous administrations, especially during the Kennedy-Johnson years, Felt wrote that he confronted Ruckelshaus, who said the president wanted the material.

"For God's sake! President or not, just tell him no!" Felt said, writing that he then turned on his heel and walked out.

On April 30, Nixon went on national television to announce that Haldeman and Ehrlichman had resigned, as had Attorney General Kleindienst. Dean had been fired. Ziegler publicly apologized to the *Post*, Carl and me.

In the middle of May I arranged to see Felt in the underground garage. He had said we could meet earlier—about 11 P.M. I expected him to be happy that Watergate was unraveling. But I also knew that he would be distressed that he had not been appointed, even temporarily, to take Gray's place. That was probably Felt's last shot.

That mid-May meeting took place in this context. It was the strangest and most alarming meeting. Felt was nervous, his jaw quivered. He raced through a series of statements and it was clear that a transformation had taken place.

First, he said, everyone's life is in danger and electronic surveillance was going on—the CIA was doing it. He said that President Nixon had personally threatened Dean. The continued effort to buy the silence of Hunt, Liddy and the five Watergate burglars, the cover-up costs, was going to be about $1 million. Most alarmingly, he said that covert activities were going on that involved the entire U.S. intelligence community.

After rattling all this off, Felt said, "That's the situation. I must go this second. You can understand. Be—well, I'll say it—be cautious." He indicated that he would soon be announcing his retirement from the FBI, and planned to leave the next month.

I went back to my apartment, called Carl and asked him to come by. Turning on music to cover the possible electronic surveillance, I typed out what Felt had said.

We took the information to Bradlee at his home, waking him at about 2 A.M. We insisted he come out on his lawn where we couldn't be bugged. I handed Bradlee a copy of my memo to read.

"What the hell do we do now?" Bradlee asked.

8

THE NEXT DAY CARL AND I GATHERED WITH THE
senior *Post* editors on the *Post's* eighth-floor roof gar-
den, three floors above the newsroom, where we presumably would be safe from eavesdropping. Richard Harwood,
then the *Post's* national editor, said he found the entire story
implausible. He questioned it all, indicating that he thought
we had finally gone around the bend and that our coverage
was nearing the edge of fantasy, a kind of paranoid delusion
of persecution.

Bradlee just wanted to know what was true, what could
be confirmed. But he did hire someone to check the phones
at the *Post*. The man also came to my apartment to check,
but no evidence of bugging or wiretapping was discovered.

That afternoon Carl and I had lunch with one of Dean's

associates who could speak authoritatively for Dean. The associate confirmed that Nixon had threatened Dean and that the cover-up costs would be $1 million.

Bradlee called another meeting—Carl, myself and the senior editors—in a vacant office in the *Post*'s fifth-floor newsroom. Many on the brightly lit newsroom floor could not contain their surprise as the senior editors, Carl and I trooped into the remote office with its glass partitions and closed the door.

We were hesitant. No one was sure what to do, so we did nothing but cover the daily story. For some time we avoided the telephones and passed notes but it soon seemed melodramatic and unnecessary. We never found any evidence that our phones were tapped or that anyone's life was in danger.

On June 22, 1973, three days before Dean went before Senator Ervin's Watergate investigating committee to charge that Nixon was involved in the illegal cover-up, Mark Felt retired from the FBI.

The momentum of Watergate continued. The Senate hearings, the disclosure of Nixon's secret White House tapes, the appointment of a special prosecutor, Archibald Cox, and his firing by Nixon in October 1973 kept Carl and me busy. There were many stories.

With Felt out of the FBI, I figured he would not be up-to-date. But in the first week in November 1973 I contacted him in order to set up a meeting in the underground garage.

It was brief. He had retired from the Bureau, but he was in touch with many friends there. That's the way the place worked. He had one simple message: One or more of the Nixon tapes contained deliberate erasures.

Carl and I wrote a story saying that there were gaps of a "suspicious nature" that "could lead someone to conclude that the tapes had been tampered with."

Ziegler flatly denied to Carl that the story was true. On the afternoon of November 21, Ziegler called Carl. Nixon's lawyers had announced in Judge Sirica's courtroom that one of the tapes contained an 18½-minute gap. "I'm giving you my word that I didn't know about this when we had our other conversation," Ziegler said.

We did not disbelieve Ziegler, and I never found out how Felt had learned this significant detail. The missing 18½-minute gap soon became a symbol for Nixon's entire Watergate problem. The truth had been deleted. The truth was missing.

But in retirement, Mark Felt faced a new series of problems and threats—all brought on by Watergate and the atmosphere that had come to pervade Washington, one he had helped create. Felt had helped light a fuse that was racing inexorably toward him.

WITH A STORY as enticing, complex, competitive and quickly unfolding as Watergate, there was little tendency or time to consider the motive of our sources. What was important was whether the information checked out and whether it was true. We were swimming, really living, in a fast-moving rapids. The cliché about drinking from a fire hose applied. There was no time to ask our sources, Why are you talking? Do you have an ax to grind? Why don't you blow the whistle publicly, stand up there and tell all you know? This was the case with Mark Felt. I was thankful for any morsel of information, confirmation or assistance he gave me while Carl and I were attempting to understand the many-headed monster of Watergate. Because of his position virtually atop the chief investigative agency, his words and guidance had immense, at times even staggering, authority. The weight, authenticity and his restraint were more important than his design, if he had one.

It was only after Nixon resigned that I began to swim up that stream seriously. Why had Felt talked when it carried substantial risks for himself and for the institution of the FBI? Had he been exposed early on, Felt would have been no hero. Technically, it was illegal to talk about grand jury information or FBI files; or it could have been made to look illegal. In retrospect, Felt had believed he was protecting the Bureau by finding a way, clandestine as it was, to push some of the information from the FBI interviews and files out to the public, to help build public and political pressure to make the president and his men answerable. The FBI findings that Watergate had many tentacles had been ignored and buried.

Second, Felt was increasingly contemptuous of the Nixon White House and its efforts to manipulate the FBI for political reasons. The young, eager-beaver patrol of White House underlings—best exemplified by John Dean—were odious to him. Felt wore a so-called Page Boy, a tiny radio receiver which emitted a high-pitched whistle when he was off duty and had to call headquarters. Often, he found, it was a call to answer some routine question from Dean or some underling. Most notorious was Lawrence Higby, Haldeman's administrative assistant, who passed on his boss's every request as if the outcome of civilization was in jeopardy if something was not done at once. Higby was so efficient that administrative assistants were known as "Higbys." At one point Higby even had his own Higby—"Higby's Higby." Higby rankled Felt particularly. Others in the government, such as Assistant Attorney General Robert Mardian (whose conviction in the Watergate cover-up was later overturned), used the White House switchboard to contact Felt, creating an aura of importance and necessity.

On Saturday morning, July 24, 1971, Felt reports in his book, Hoover himself called to say that Felt was to go to the White House to help Egil Krogh, a White House aide who was supervising Hunt and Liddy's Plumber operation to stop leaks. Krogh wanted the FBI to polygraph suspected leakers. Hoover had seven years earlier ordered the FBI not to use the lie detector. Felt described a series of White

House meetings to chase down leakers because Nixon was "climbing the walls."

Third, his reverence for Hoover and strict Bureau procedure made Pat Gray's appointment as director all the more shocking. Felt had obviously concluded he was the logical successor to Hoover and instead this naive, easily manipulated former submariner and Justice Department political hack had been put in charge of the FBI.

Fourth, Felt liked the game. His first real Bureau expertise was as a World War II spy hunter. Converting all that knowledge and tradecraft to become an agent runner was perhaps natural. I suspect that in his mind I was his agent. He beat it into my head: secrecy at all cost, no loose talk, no talk about him at all, no indication to anyone that such a secret source existed.

In *All the President's Men*, Carl and I said that we had speculated on Deep Throat's piecemeal approach to providing information. "If he told everything he knew all at once, a good Plumber might be able to find the leak. By making the reporters go elsewhere to fill out his information, he minimized his risk. Perhaps. But it was equally possible that he felt that the effect of one or two big stories, no matter how devastating, could be blunted by the White House. Or, by raising the stakes gradually, was he simply making the game more interesting for himself? The reporters tended to doubt that someone in his position would be so cavalier toward matters affecting Richard Nixon or the Presidency itself. More likely, they thought, Deep Throat was trying to protect the office, to effect a change in its conduct before all was lost." Each time I had raised the question Felt had gravely insisted, "I have to do this my way."

WITH FELT RETIRED, I worried that Carl and I would be handicapped. Though Watergate special prosecutor Archibald Cox was in charge of the ongoing investigation, the FBI was still doing lots of the spadework.

"The problem was that we wouldn't burglarize," Felt told me in a phone conversation during July 1973, a month after his retirement. John Ehrlichman had testified before the Senate Watergate Committee that the Plumbers team of Hunt and Liddy had burglarized the office of Daniel Ellsberg's psychiatrist because the FBI and its director at the time in 1971, J. Edgar Hoover, refused to conduct a vigorous investigation of Ellsberg. "Those fellows were going out as substitutes for the FBI," Ehrlichman had testified.

Felt was boiling about the Ehrlichman testimony, and I eventually coaxed him to go on the record defending the FBI's Ellsberg investigation. It was a giant step forward. Carl and I wrote a 15-paragraph story for the inside of the *Post* that ran on July 28, 1973, quoting him. It was headlined, "Ex-FBI Aide Defends Ellsberg Investigation." Pictures of Felt and Hoover ran with the story. I had visions of Felt mellowing in retirement and soon telling me what was in the bottom of the FBI–CIA–Nixon administration secrets barrel.

IN THE FALL OF 1972, as we were writing critical Watergate stories, Carl and I had signed a book contract with Simon & Schuster. The publisher was going to pay us a total of $55,000, a large sum of money for us at the time. Our proposed outline said we planned a conventional narrative about the actions of Nixon, his White House, Mitchell, Howard Hunt and Gordon Liddy. But the next year was filled with so many new developments—the Ellsberg burglary, the secret White House tapes, the appointment of Cox and his wide-ranging grand jury investigations—that we got little or nothing written.

On a Sunday in August of 1973, Carl and I had brunch outside at a restaurant near Dupont Circle. We were fretting, knowing we had to get our book done but wanting to stay on the story, which was yielding fresh revelations weekly, if not daily. What were our options? The book was due at the end of the year. I recall trying the draft of a chapter that began with Nixon's January 20, 1973, inaugural—triumphant on the surface but grim underneath because Watergate was about to burst open. But new developments were changing the story almost daily, rendering a serious narrative about this sweeping and snowballing story virtually impossible. At least for us. We had never written a book. Carl, at age 28, already had nine years of remarkable newspaper writing behind him. I had my unpublishable undergraduate novel under my belt (where it would stay and where it belonged).

We decided we had no alternative but to write the story of covering Watergate as *Post* reporters. It was what we knew best. Write what you know, what you have experienced, is one of the rules. My mother had a house in Naples, Florida, that she and my stepfather only used in the winter. She agreed to let us use it for six weeks. We packed all our notes, files, memos, old story drafts, published stories and other clips and headed for Florida. We felt like we were running out on the story but the *Post* editors agreed to give us time off as long as we remained in touch.

My mother's house was a single-story rancher on a waterway not far from the Gulf of Mexico. Carl wrote outside by the pool each day, and I in a room next to the kitchen. We agreed to try to write 10 pages a day each recounting our personal experiences from the reporting we had done in covering the story, the interaction with the editors, and the eventual decision to publish the main stories. By the end of six weeks we had more than 500 manuscript pages—the core of what became *All the President's Men*. We contacted several of our unnamed sources to ask if we could identify them by name in the book. Hugh Sloan, the Nixon campaign treasurer, for example, had been an unnamed source in the newspaper stories, but he agreed to let us use his name for the book.

I called Felt and asked, very gingerly, that since he was now retired, and since he had let me quote him on the record defending the FBI, would he consider letting me identify him for the book?

He exploded. Absolutely not. Was I mad even to make such a request? He went further, suggesting at one point that he didn't know what I was talking about, as if he might be taping the call to create deniability. It was about as emphatic a no as anyone could receive. Angry and unhappy, he told me, Don't call here again. As I stayed on the line with some more questions he calmed down, telling me that he had to be able to count on our agreement, to count on me. He used the word "inviolate."

Our agreement was that there would be no identification of him, his agency or even a suggestion in print that such a source existed. Nonetheless, during the previous year, Carl and I had made numerous references in print to FBI files. On one occasion I had quoted Felt anonymously as a source saying that the funding of Watergate was "a Haldeman operation." Felt had never objected to these references, and I had thought it gave me some leeway.

More was at stake than I might realize, he said, again casting a mystery, suggesting a still wide chasm between his knowledge and mine. That had always been the basis of our relationship: He knew and I didn't. I would flounder, fall dangerously off course, and he would right the ship of knowledge. And apparently it would always be such.

Felt made me feel shame. I wondered how I could even have made such a request. Certainly he had made represen-tations to his colleagues at the FBI, the club, and to his friends and family that he had not been a Watergate source for us. Exposure would challenge his probity with everyone important in his life. He still had potential legal liability. But most important, Nixon was still president. The Watergate cover-up was continuing, and Nixon still seemed determined to plug leaks. Felt's contribution had been sufficiently under the radar that no one other than Carl, me, a few other re-porters vaguely and the *Post* editors, even knew there was a secret high-level source that was an underpinning for some of our stories.

Felt certainly did not know that those of us at the *Post* re-ferred to him as Deep Throat. The nickname Simons gave him had stuck. I guess I wondered at the time what Felt might think about being named after one of the most graphic pornographic movies of the day.

But since Felt was called Deep Throat at the *Post*, we called him Deep Throat in the book. We held nothing back. Carl and I laid out what happened—the good stories, the bad stories, the goofs—exactly as it occurred.

We finished the book in December 1973 and publication was set for the spring of 1974. I was so relieved just to have it finished that I stopped thinking about it. Sales, reviews, reactions or the prospect of a movie were all vague. During the beginning of 1974 it was still not clear what the Watergate endgame might be. Nixon was in serious trouble, Cox had been fired on Nixon's orders, an impeachment investigation by the House Judiciary Committee was underway, and a new special prosecutor, Leon Jaworski, was thundering on. But no one, including Carl and me, had specific knowledge about what might be on the White House tapes and the damage they would do. I had some dark inklings, and Carl was pretty sure they would be bad, very bad.

We closed *All the President's Men* with Nixon's annual State of the Union address January 30, 1974, to a joint session of the House and Senate in which he said forcefully, "One year of Watergate is enough."

He had added defiantly, "I want you to know that I have no intention whatever of ever walking away from the job that the American people elected me to do."

In other words, he was not going to resign. No way. Everyone knew that Nixon had extraordinary survival skills. He certainly was no quitter.

BEFORE OUR BOOK was even written, movie actor Robert Redford called me at the *Post,* introduced himself, and recalled being on the campaign bus with some reporters in 1972. He talked about our Watergate stories—how bold, accusatory, refreshing and suspect they were all in one. Redford said he appreciated how the stories scratched the paranoid itch the liberal Democratic establishment had about Nixon. Later as the evidence of their truth emerged, Redford said, he thought that the really interesting Watergate story was the story of Carl's and my work—the struggle, doubt and process of producing stories that took on the president. Redford's ideas no doubt contributed to the idea of telling the story as a personal one about journalism. It never really crossed my mind to leave out the details of Deep Throat's role. It was important, and in all respects for me, the most personal and human.

AS I WOULD ONLY LEARN LATER, on February 25, 1974, an attorney in the office of the Watergate special prosecutor summoned Felt for an interview.

"You realize that you might have violated the law," the young prosecutor said, according to Felt's account in his book. The prosecutor would not explain how or when. They put Felt before the grand jury. The prosecutors were trying to nail Pat Gray on a perjury charge, and they wanted Felt to remember handing him a memo describing how Kissinger had ordered wiretaps on 17 White House aides and reporters. Felt said he couldn't say for sure. His initial "F" was not on the memo. They accused him of trying to protect Gray, not knowing how laughable that was. "You are lying!" the prosecutor shouted. Felt was incredulous at the amateurism, the tough-guy lawyer treatment, and offended that a former senior FBI official would be shown no more courtesy than a Mafioso.

9

---

*A*LL THE PRESIDENT'S MEN WAS PUBLISHED IN APRIL 1974. The first weekend it was out I recall riding in a car and tuning to the local news radio station, WTOP. I listened in amazement for some 10 to 15 minutes as they did a nonstop reading, mainly from the detailed sections about my meetings with the unidentified Deep Throat. The book shot to No. 1 on the national bestseller lists. Carl and I tried to keep our heads down, continuing to write stories about the latest Watergate developments for the *Post*.

I vividly recall phoning Felt after the book was released. I was dying to know what he thought. Certainly he had seen it or heard about it. When he heard my voice, he hung up. For days I was haunted, imagining the worst. The worst ranged from the possibility that he might take his own life to the higher likelihood that he would go public and denounce me as a betrayer and scum who had exploited our accidental friendship. Or he might claim I had described our relationship or some information inaccurately. After all, only he and I knew.

I can still hear the bang of his telephone and the sudden dial tone. Hanging up was worse than any words he might have uttered. I wanted to know what he was thinking, but I did not have the courage to phone him again. What was the storm he was living? I wondered. How much was directed at me?

In June, *Washingtonian* magazine published a story saying Felt was the most likely candidate to be Deep Throat, reasoning that he had motive, opportunity, access, knew the methods for clandestine meetings and was offended by Nixon and his men.

On June 25, *The Wall Street Journal* did one of their signature tongue-in-cheek front page feature stories headlined: "If You Drink Scotch, Smoke, Read, Maybe You're Deep Throat." It began, "W. Mark Felt says he isn't now, nor has he ever been Deep Throat. Of course, says the former acting associate director of the FBI, if he really were Deep Throat, you'd hardly expect him to admit it, now would you? Not that he is, Mr. Felt quickly adds."

Felt told the *Journal* reporter that he didn't disagree with the reasoning that it was he. "But I do disagree with the conclusion. Because I'm just not that kind of person." I re-call reading that quote. It left me cringing. Felt told the *Journal* he thought that Deep Throat was a "composite." He was the first person I know of to float that theory—another false trail and superb cover for Deep Throat.

I now know from Felt's book and the records that in June 1974, two FBI agents arrived at his front door to interview him. One of the agents was Angelo Lano, whom Felt had never met, but Lano had been the chief FBI Watergate in-vestigator during 1972 in the Washington field office. In-stead of asking the questions at his home, Lano and the other agent said the interview would be done at a nearby Holiday Inn. Felt suspected this meant the interview would be secretly recorded. As a normal courtesy given his former high rank, he expected to be questioned at the FBI in the office of the current director, Clarence Kelley.

At the motel Lano advised Felt of his constitutional rights and asked him to sign the form acknowledging that his rights had been read to him. Felt signed without read-ing it. Lano was indignant at this, and Felt said he had gone through this with more subjects than Lano would ever know.

The investigation was about a leak of Segretti FBI docu-ments to *The New York Times*. Felt denied any involvement. The drip, drip, drip of inquiry and the investigative zeal of the era were coming home to roost, and Felt didn't like it one bit. Though I didn't know it at the time, Felt was carrying around a secret that was perhaps as big or bigger than his role as Deep Throat.

Nixon announced his resignation the night of August 8, 1974. I was tempted to call Felt, just to check in, get his reaction, thank him or whatever. Couldn't we now talk it through? Maybe we could be civilized and meet at his house. After all, we had both, in our own ways, been right about Nixon, hadn't we? Having been Deep Throat should not be a shroud. But I didn't want to get the hang-up treatment again. I dreaded that. A call might unleash something—feelings of double cross or exposure, rage, disappointment—that for the moment seemed safely bottled up or at least dormant. But the nagging incompleteness of the relationship was painful for me.

Carl and I took another leave from the *Post* to write a book on Nixon's last year in office and the story of the collapse of his presidency, which we titled *The Final Days*. The focus was on Nixon, his lawyers and White House staff. Neither Deep Throat nor Mark Felt was mentioned.

Felt's reward during this period continued to be the FBI investigation into the suspicion that he had leaked FBI documents about Donald Segretti to *New York Times* reporter John Crewdson.

At *The Washington Post* we ran a front page story about the Felt investigation that was written by *Los Angeles Times* reporter Ronald J. Ostrow on November 17, 1974—three months after Nixon's resignation. Ostrow was one of the best Justice Department reporters around, and the *Post* editors trusted his work.

So it was an *L.A. Times* story in *The Washington Post* about an investigation leaked to *The New York Times.* Perfect.

Ostrow interviewed Felt and quoted him as saying that the investigation was probably a result of the *Washingtonian* article which had fingered him as the leading Deep Throat suspect. "Because of the Deep Throat allegation," Felt wrote in his book, "they [the FBI] said, 'Well it must have been Felt who gave Crewdson all the papers.' But I did not leak any information to Woodward or Bernstein. I'm not Deep Throat. I did not leak any information to Crewdson. I did not give him any documents. And I think the whole thing is ridiculous and insulting."

In 1975, Felt was called to testify five times before the Senate committee investigating intelligence agency abuses. In a separate matter, on two occasions FBI agents called on him in an investigation of Bureau corruption. He had to admit that he had attended some dinners for the heads of various foreign intelligence services that had been paid for from FBI money. He also "confessed," as he put it sarcastically in his book, to having the FBI exhibits section make some picture frames for him to display photos of Hoover, the attorney general and others for his office wall. He had to appear in public before a House committee chaired by Representative Bella Abzug, the New York Democrat, to testify about Hoover's confidential files. And so it went, humiliation piled on top of humiliation.

Felt was becoming a professional witness. He knew enough about investigations to realize that a witness who had seen so much, been there at critical moments, eventually had to have done something. The witness sooner or later becomes the defendant.

There is a memo, dated March 25, 1975, in the FBI files that shows how much *All the President's Men* rankled the FBI. R. E. Long, one senior official, wrote to another asking whether it was possible to disclose "some information from the Watergate investigation aimed at restoring to the FBI any prestige lost during that investigation. Such information could also serve to dispel the false impression left by the book *All the President's Men* that its authors, Carl Bernstein and Bob Woodward, not the FBI, solved the Watergate case.

"... a comparison of the chronology of our investigation with the events cited in *All the President's Men* will show we were substantially and constantly ahead of these *Washington Post* investigative reporters. In essence, they were interviewing the same people we had interviewed but subsequent to our interviews and often after the interviewee had testified before the grand jury. The difference, which contributes

such great pressure, it was difficult to figure out what was going on because everybody was against us, because people were whispering to Katharine Graham that they'll ruin her newspaper."

That's some of what the movie captured—the uncertainty and doubt. Most of the sources and informants were low-level players who saw just a piece of the conspiracies. Director Alan J. Pakula picked actor Hal Holbrook to play Deep Throat. Holbrook was the wise actor of the era, cerebral and high-minded. He was the one who seemingly knew the entire story but wouldn't tell it all. It was a powerful performance, capturing the authoritative and seasoned intensity, cynicism and gruffness of the man in the underground garage.

In a long February 16, 2001, article in *The New York Times* by Rick Lyman, director Steven Soderbergh, who won the Best Director Oscar for *Traffic,* watched *All the President's Men* and explained why it is one of his favorites:

"The scenes are just mind-boggling," Mr. Soderbergh said. "Everything about them. The way they're lit. The way they're shot. The dialogue. The sound.

"Woodward wanders through the dark garage, his footfalls hitting like bricks on the otherwise hushed soundtrack. A droning air conditioner hums in the background. Finally, up against a pillar several yards away, he sees a dark figure (Hal Holbrook) illuminated by the orange flash of a cigarette being lighted. Cold and warm colors mixing again.

"It's just so perfect," Mr. Soderbergh said. At a cursory glance, the scene appears lost in gloom and colorlessness. But there are exceptionally subtle varieties of color and texture.

"In his close-ups Holbrook's got a light right in his eyes, but it's maybe two stops down, at the very edge of perception," Mr. Soderbergh said. It does give the actor the look of an animal hiding in the forest at night, or a vampire. "And there is another light off to the side that just draws a line right around him, highlighting the side of his face. Look at him. He's like a ghost."

But when Mr. Redford appears to deliver his half of the lines, the look is quite different. Though still clothed in gloom, slightly warmer colors illuminate his face. "See, with Redford we get skin tones, but with Holbrook it's just completely monochromatic. Deep Throat is not even human."

The Deep Throat sequences "are so beautifully constructed," Mr. Soderbergh said. "The power dynamic between the two of them is so very well drawn. No, I think they are really the heart of the movie."

This was written 25 years after the movie was released, and I don't agree that the Deep Throat scenes are really the heart of the movie. I told Pakula that he would have to fig-ure out how to do these scenes. I had put all I knew in the book and was not going to show him the specific under-ground garage. But the scenes in the movie capture the tur-bulence of the relationship. More important, the scenes pose the critical questions in journalism. How much can a re-porter penetrate to the inside? How close can a reporter really, truly and fully learn what goes on? Deep Throat was someone who knew—an informant from the inside—yet someone who dramatizes the limits of journalism. There is no truth serum. Informants play by their own rules. The best informants don't tell by what rules they are playing.

When the movie came out—it premiered at the Kennedy Center—the reviews were generally strong. Roger Ebert said Holbrook "is disturbingly detached, almost as if he's observing the events with a hollow laugh." *Time* maga-zine put the movie on its cover. "Hal Holbrook is brilliant as Deep Throat, giving him an arrogance and condescen-sion that makes the famous non-person's behavior explic-able."

Arrogance! Condescension! Yet explicable behavior! I was looking for a way to plow through the layers of this neurotic and paranoid friendship. I was tempted to call Felt and see what he thought. Maybe I should do one of my show-up-on-his-doorstep routines? Perhaps being played by Holbrook in a dramatically heroic role would melt the iceberg that had risen between us. Or was the iceberg still growing?

But I was basically gutless. I did nothing.

WHAT I DIDN'T KNOW THEN was that Mark Felt was in big legal trouble and he badly needed to preserve his law enforcement ties. For the six years before his death in May 1972, Hoover had prohibited the use of the so-called black-bag jobs, or surreptitious break-ins, to gather intelligence in domestic security cases. That changed with the rise of the Weather Underground Organization (WUO). The Weathermen were generally considered the most radical and violence-prone of the domestic activists or terrorists. There was some evidence that the Weathermen had connections with foreign governments, and the group had taken responsibility for the 1971 bombing of the Capitol and the 1972 bombing of the Pentagon. On July 18, 1972, Gray had written a note to Felt saying of the WUO, "Hunt to exhaustion. No holds barred."

Felt, who—as I knew as well as anyone—was inclined to take matters into his own hands, concluded that this meant the FBI break-ins could begin again. At the time I did not understand the Vietnam-era near-hysteria he apparently felt about the Weather Underground. He would later begin his 1979 book by stating, "In the late Sixties and early Seventies, the country was at war—civil war—but only a few knew it. The Weather Underground, Cuban-taught, self-proclaimed Communist Revolutionaries, publicly declared war on the United States." The book is filled with some over-the-top comments about this group. Adopting almost a domestic version of President George W. Bush's preemptive war doctrine, Felt provided this justification for the break-ins and for suspending the Fourth Amendment: "It is the function of the FBI to prevent violence and other subversive acts rather than to wait until the bomb has exploded."

Felt and Edward S. Miller, the head of FBI intelligence, decided to authorize break-ins by special FBI teams. Clandestine entries into the homes or offices of relatives and friends of Weathermen fugitives seemed a good way to develop leads for locating them. On at least five occasions, Felt approved black-bag jobs—FBI break-ins—without consulting Gray.

IN THE SUMMER OF 1976, stories began appearing, first from the resourceful Ron Ostrow of the L.A. *Times,* reporting that the Justice Department was investigating whether the FBI had violated the civil rights of associates of Weathermen political activists who were American citizens, protected by the Fourth Amendment of the Constitution, which prohibits unreasonable search and seizure. The investigation first focused on some 125 present or former FBI agents who were interrogated or given immunity from prosecution. It grew out of the post-Watergate inclination to inquire into any possible abuse of government power, especially potential violations of the civil rights of anti-Vietnam groups and Nixon critics.

"It was perfectly obvious that I would be the eventual target of this form of arm-twisting," Felt wrote in his book.

The FBI burglaries were a big story that summer of 1976 with all the overtones of Watergate. So I jumped into the fray. Carl had left the paper to write a book about his family.

Another reporter at the *Post*, Bruce Howard, and I spoke with Felt and Ed Miller. Both said that Pat Gray had authorized the Weathermen burglaries. Felt was willing to talk on the record so we quoted him in the paper. "I'm convinced that I was acting with his approval," Felt said of Gray. "I have the impression strongly. . . . I'm not prepared to say exactly what Gray said, but I believe I can reconstruct it."

This was a less than definitive statement, but Felt was in an unusual mood and he said he would approve these burglaries if he had it to do over again. "I'm proud of what I did." He went on about how violent the Weathermen had been. "You've got to remember that we were dealing with murderers, terrorists, people who were responsible for mass destruction . . . the key word is violence. They were planning mass destruction. . . . Please emphasize the viciousness of these people. We were dealing with fanatics.

"If you learn in advance of a bomb about to go off, you can't put your fingers in your ears and wait for it to go off." He conceded that the burglaries hadn't turned up information that led to the capture of the fugitive Weathermen. "But these people had claimed responsibility for hundreds of bombings and we wanted to put them out of circulation . . . we had an obligation to.

"I think I have observed the spirit and the letter of the Constitution . . . the right of one person cannot be allowed to exist to the detriment of hundreds."

I published all this. It was odd, a bit of a charade. Felt was apparently developing a theory to justify his actions. And he was obviously worried that he might be indicted and jailed at age 63.

As I continued to report the story, I tracked down former Attorney General Richard Kleindienst, who said that he had told Pat Gray that no surreptitious entries were authorized. I wrote a front page story on August 27, 1976, that undercut part of Felt's defense that he had high-level authority for the break-ins. Kleindienst was going to say it elsewhere, so I didn't feel that my reporting added to Felt's troubles.

The next time I talked to him, however, he was furious and icy. He had strong beliefs. He quotes Thomas Jefferson in his book, "The laws of necessity, of self-preservation, of saving our country when it is danger, are of higher obligation. To lose our country by a scrupulous adherence to the written law, would be to lose law itself."

So Felt had taken the law into his own hands. It was civil disobedience, a somewhat novel argument for a former law enforcement officer. He was also arguing that the break-ins were legal. He strongly believed the investigation was a grave injustice. I could clearly see why he didn't want to come forward and announce that, by the way, he had been Deep Throat.

For the next two years he waited. "My wife and my family were subjected to the fears and anxieties of what my fate would bring," he wrote.

10

———

DURING 1976, WHEN I WAS REPORTING THE FBI break-in story, I had lunch with a senior Justice Department official. It was a highly confidential, off-the-record discussion. But in 2005 he released me and agreed to go on the record. The official was Stanley Pottinger, the assistant attorney general heading the civil rights division. He was in charge of the grand jury investigation into the FBI break-ins.

Sitting in a downtown Washington, D.C., restaurant in 1976, Pottinger said that something strange had happened when Mark Felt had testified before the grand jury.

I stiffened, certainly telegraphing my discomfort.

Pottinger said that Felt was asked if the Nixon White House had pressed the FBI to conduct the black-bag jobs.

Felt denied any pressure but volunteered with a smile

that he was such a frequent visitor at the White House that some people thought he was Deep Throat. After Pottinger and the other Justice lawyers were finished with their interrogation, Pottinger, as was the custom, asked if any grand jurors, who are ordinary citizens, had questions for the witness. One man raised his hand and asked, "Were you?"

"Was I what?" Felt inquired.

"Were you Deep Throat?"

Felt looked so stunned, Pottinger said, he seemed to go white. Listening to this over lunch, I probably went white as well.

"No," Felt initially answered.

Continuing his story, Pottinger said he stood up abruptly and instructed the stenographer to stop taking notes for the record. He then walked over to the witness chair and whispered to Felt, "You are under oath, so you have to answer truthfully. On the other hand, I consider the question to be outside the bounds of our official investigation, so if you prefer, I'll withdraw the question. What would you like me to do?"

Flushed, Felt very rapidly requested, "Withdraw the question."

Pottinger, smiling broadly at me, said he formally withdrew both question and answer, adding ominously that it was all he needed. Obviously Felt had been the secret source.

I was jumping out of my skin, but trying to keep a poker

face. Pottinger remembers that I did some kind of dance—trying not to affirm or deny. At one point later, Pottinger recalls that I even babbled something like, "Well, just because someone might be a source doesn't necessarily make them Deep Throat" or "A source himself might think he's Deep Throat even if he's not." I hope I did not go to such extremes and utter such absurdities, and I don't believe I did. But I was profoundly worried that his identity would get out. Felt's trust in me was already shaken after all that had been written about our meetings in *All the President's Men*. He must have worried they would try to get him on perjury about Deep Throat. Overall, I realized he must have felt dangerously exposed.

Pottinger said he would not tell anyone. But with something like this—too good not to repeat—even given the strict grand jury secrecy rules, I was convinced the story would get out in some form. It had to, and I held my breath waiting for the unmasking at any moment. I did not want to attempt to extract a promise from Pottinger because that would only give him confirmation, though from the smile on his face it was clear he was convinced.

The next summer, 1977, I was in Hyannisport, Massachusetts, as a weekend guest at the home of Ethel Kennedy, widow of late Attorney General Robert Kennedy. When I walked into dinner one night, there was Stan Pottinger. I felt as if the ghost of Banquo was on the scene and I eyed him uncomfortably. The Kennedy dinner table was a forum for gossip and tales of intrigue, and anyone with a really good story would be treated to a round of boisterous applause and laughter. And Pottinger had a potential show-stopper. I felt a growing sense of dread as the wine and conversation flowed. Senator Edward M. Kennedy was there also, in competition with Ethel to draw out the guests.

But most eyes were on Jackie Kennedy, widow of President Kennedy, who was next to Pottinger. I sat across from them. It was the first time I had met Jackie Kennedy, who in her gentle, vulnerable voice made it clear that the Watergate exposé was about the best thing to have happened in years. She was familiar with the book and movie of *All the President's Men,* and she had many comments and questions.

So who was Deep Throat? the former first lady inquired.

I froze. Pottinger recalls that I said something along the lines of, "Stan thinks he knows, don't you?" I hope I was more careful, and I believe I was.

Pottinger, a very handsome man with long hair, stared me down and burst into a smile that enveloped his face and said something innocuous. There was a long silence, followed by the disappointed groans of the other guests. It was soon clear the ribaldry of the Kennedy dinner table in summer would not extract the identity of Deep Throat.

Pottinger later said he thought my question to him was a

way of testing him. When he didn't answer in that environment, he thought, I would be satisfied he would stay quiet. I was never fully satisfied, but to his eternal credit he kept the secret for nearly three decades. In 2005, he told me that he believed it critical that reporters be able to maintain confidential sources for as long as necessary, and he did not want to play any part whatsoever in a premature exposure of Felt. Pottinger added, "His ambivalence underscores the gravity of what he felt. It must not have been easy. In my opinion he made the right judgment to provide you with information but it was probably against all his instincts. And that is the hardest thing for any human being to do."

ON APRIL 10, 1978, a federal grand jury indicted Gray, Felt and Miller, charging that they did "unlawfully, willfully and knowingly combine, conspire, confederate and agree together and with each other to injure and oppress citizens of the United States who were relatives and acquaintances of the Weathermen fugitives." It was a big front page story in the *Post*.

Sometime afterward, I reached Felt by phone. He sounded worn, tired. There was a hesitation in his voice, that of a man facing jail, probably the last place he thought he would wind up. The felony indictment meant that if convicted he could be punished with a prison sentence of up to 10 years or a $10,000 fine or both.

I said I was truly sorry that it had come to this.

He sounded, or acted, as if he did not recognize my name or my voice, as if I were some stranger or caller voicing sympathy.

"Thank you," he said with a dry edge to his voice.

I tried to break through, saying something like, "Bob Woodward, Bob Woodward, you know, from *The Washington Post*?"

I believe he groaned.

Repeating myself, I said I was sorry. I realized that I was only trouble in his life. I had wanted to see if there was some way to square his disgust with Nixon's break-ins and his own actions. Hadn't he taken the national security worry too far? I wanted to ask. But he was in no mood to talk or spar with me. I said goodbye.

I didn't have a strong opinion about the Weathermen break-ins. Breaking and entering on the off chance that some relative or friend might have left a phone number or address of one of the fugitives seemed extreme.

For some time I had a fantasy that I could convince Felt to let me tell the full story of his role as Deep Throat. Many people, perhaps most people, would see him as a hero. He could explain what he had done and why. Public opinion might be with him. I even had the idea that I could testify at his trial as a character witness, showing up dramatically, taking the oath and laying out his willingness to blow the whistle on Nixon, the Justice Department, Gray and others. This was a courageous man, right? But I realized I wasn't sure. Lurking around in an underground parking garage, insisting on anonymity, often refusing to supply specifics, hiding and lying to colleagues, friends and family—all courageous, right? I found myself worrying about him, and my feelings verged on pity because he had submerged who he was.

But again I figured this was also a calculation on his part. If he were unmasked or if he unmasked himself, how might he explain the evident contradictions? He had staked so much on not being Deep Throat. Where would the honor be? Who would believe him on other matters? He would be in effect a perjured witness. I suspect he saw the trap. The only safety was in consistency. He had chosen his course.

When he talked there was barely any of the snap, insight or humor I had seen and been drawn to. Ten days after the indictment, Felt, Gray and Miller appeared at the Federal District Courthouse in downtown D.C. for arraignment. I thought of going but decided I had better not. He might see me and lash out. There was no guarantee what he might do or say. Felt's statement to *The Wall Street Journal* stuck in my mind: "I'm just not that kind of person." Did he know who he was? Did I? His denials seemed to be embedded in the identity he had fashioned for himself. He was like a witness who had told his story a dozen or a hundred times. He had to stick to it, and over the years, he had perhaps even come to believe it.

The police estimated that some 1,200 current and former FBI agents gathered at a silent vigil of support for Felt and the others on their arraignment day.

In his book Felt wrote that he hoped the chapter on his indictment didn't come off as bitter, and that the published version eliminated some of his stronger language from earlier drafts. "I am angry and frustrated, yes—but not bitter." There didn't seem to be an abundance of self-knowledge in this remark. He was in a rage. I wondered what his thinking might be about the connection between the Watergate disclosures in which he had played no small part, his indictment and the possibility of prison.

FELT PUBLISHED HIS BOOK, The FBI Pyramid, in 1979, before his trial. The inside flap said, "Mark Felt, who was rumored to be the famous informer Deep Throat . . ."

How odd, I thought, that he would allow himself to be identified "rumored to be the famous informer," and then to categorically deny it in the book.

I bought a copy of The FBI Pyramid—$12.95 was the going price for a hardback. It didn't have an index, and of course I read it carefully. Not until page 225 did Felt address the question of providing information to me. In early 1973 Gray conveyed to Felt that Attorney General Dick

Kleindienst had told him that Felt might have to go. "I might have to get rid of you," Gray said. "He says White House staff members are convinced that you are the FBI source of leaks to Woodward and Bernstein."

"Pat," Felt said he replied, "I haven't leaked anything to anybody. They are wrong!"

"I believe you," Gray replied, "but the White House doesn't. Kleindienst has told me on three or four occasions to get rid of you but I refused. He didn't say this came from higher up but I am convinced that it did."

Felt concluded, "This disclosure came as an unpleasant surprise. . . . I could feel the anger rising in me but I was very appreciative of Gray's indication of support." On the question of possible motive, he wrote that it was true he would have liked to have been appointed FBI director after Hoover's death, but denied he was jealous of Gray. "I never leaked information to Woodward and Bernstein or to anyone else!"

I wondered if he was trying to be literally true—he had never leaked to "Woodward and Bernstein." He had never met Carl. His dealings were only with me. He was scrupulous about staying away from specifics in FBI files. I suspect he did not consider that he was "leaking" information—he was only supposed to confirm what I had and steer me. But the sum of all the confirmations and guidance added up to more than a leak. It was a road map.

Later in the book, Felt noted that Haldeman stated in a television interview that he thought Felt had been Deep Throat. But, Felt noted, Haldeman later changed his mind and believed the source had been Fred Fielding, John Dean's deputy White House counsel.

Felt also noted that the White House tapes showed that Nixon thought Felt was providing information to us.

I don't recall seeing a review, or ever being asked about the book. It disappeared. I was a little jarred that he would make such a categorical denial, but the more I reflected, I realized that he was focused on his trial.

What followed for Felt and the others was a tedious legal battle about what could be disclosed before a jury and the public over these break-ins. Was it high national security or illegal abuse of police power? Operations were given code names like "Program C," supposedly to protect national security. It was a legal morass. Prosecutors decided to give Pat Gray a separate trial. Felt and Miller would be tried together, and first. In the fall of 1980, at the federal courthouse in Washington, D.C., the trial opened before a jury of eight women and four men who were to be sequestered for however long it took.

Wednesday, October 29, 1980, was an extraordinary day in the trial. As the *Post* reporter, Laura A. Kiernan, wrote, the 67-year-old witness had a familiar face and hair, a "powdered ghostly look."

After taking the oath swearing to tell the whole truth, the witness sat down and said he was retired.

"Were you once the president of the United States?" the prosecutor inquired.

"Yes," said Nixon. He had been called by the prosecutors. Nixon had volunteered to appear—the first and only time he would testify in a trial after resigning. He recounted how he had approved the 1970 Huston plan that would have permitted surreptitious entries in national security cases. Though it was rescinded four days later, Nixon said he was anxious that the Weathermen fugitives be captured because there was "hard evidence" they had foreign government connections.

It was a maddening 45 minutes of testimony because Nixon was not asked whether he had approved the five break-ins that Felt and Ed Miller authorized. He seemed to side with Felt, because as president he believed he had authority to order break-ins if the national security was threatened and he had delegated that authority to the FBI director. Though Huston had said in a memo to the president that the "black-bag jobs" were "clearly illegal," Nixon said that the good cause of protecting the national security overrode such considerations. A presidential authorization, Nixon claimed, meant that "what would otherwise be unlawful or illegal becomes legal."

This was the very attitude that got Nixon in trouble on

Watergate, and he made these declarations pounding his finger on the wooden bench in front of him.

Frequently lecturing, Nixon said that international terrorism with assassinations, murders and bombings was a grave threat requiring extraordinary action. "We are concerned it might happen here," he added nearly 21 years before the September 11, 2001, terrorist attacks in the United States. He reminded the jury of the Vietnam War. "All these concerns, I can assure you as one who went through it, were greatly magnified—I guess that's the proper word—by the fact that in 1969, 1970, 1971, we were at war.

"I can assure that I think that, I hope that neither President Carter or Governor Reagan if he should be president has to do what I had to do, what Franklin Roosevelt had to do—"

The judge interrupted and directed the lawyer to ask his next question.

Nixon would have none of that and he continued, "what President Truman had to do, that is, write letters to people whose sons have been killed in war."

His message on the witness stand was supportive of Felt's and Miller's argument that they had presidential authority, though it had not been expressly given.

Other than the suspicions expressed on the White House tapes that Felt had helped Carl and me, I have no idea if Nixon thought he was, in effect, testifying on behalf of one of his betrayers. I suspect the testimony was part of Nixon's efforts to stage a comeback and show that his national security concerns were valid. I was astonished to read about his testimony, but I certainly gave no thought to trying to contact Felt. In his time of profound personal jeopardy, I belonged, and stayed, in the background.

On November 6, 1980—just a week later—after eight hours of deliberations following the two-month trial, the jury found Felt and Miller guilty of conspiring to violate the civil rights of those whose homes were burglarized. Outside the courthouse, Felt said, "I spent my entire adult life working for the government and I always tried to do what I thought was right and what was in the best interest of this country and what would protect the safety of this country. Obviously, the jury didn't agree with me."

Three days later the *Post* had a Sunday editorial which of course I, as a reporter, didn't see in advance. The editorial said the prosecution was "essential," and said the case is "a landmark that should deter future policemen from overreaching their legal authority."

I finally got up the nerve to call Felt and once again told him how sorry I was about the jury verdict.

He said that Richard Nixon had done more to assist him than *The Washington Post*.

What do you mean? I inquired.

He mentioned the editorial.

I attempted to explain that I had nothing to do with the editorials, and that the *Post's* policy was that no one from the newsroom could have any influence over editorials.

He scoffed at the mention of *Post* policy.

I was not involved or notified, I protested.

I hope the irony is not lost on you, he said, reminding me of my commitment not to further exploit our relationship—I believe that was the way he put it.

The point was not lost on me, I said.

Felt said he was counting on me to remain silent. It was more important than ever. He was facing 10 years in jail, and expected he could be sentenced to several years. He said his wife, Audrey, was sick and he was taking care of her.

Now, I recall beginning, might be the time—

Oh no, it's not, he said sharply, firmly and loudly.

But— I started.

NO.

He had apparently concluded that his defense was that he was on the side of law enforcement, playing by the rules and procedures of national security. Running off to a parking garage to talk to me at 2 A.M. would subject him to the charge that he was out of control, a freelancer, inclined to take things into his own hands for a larger purpose that he, and he alone, defined. He seemed to fear that he would be considered a snitch, a rat.

For me, Watergate had been a cleansing. For him, it was becoming the opposite. The two of us saw his actions and their results so differently, I realized, but any reflections on the unfairness of it only added to my growing feelings of personal responsibility for his plight.

NIXON PUBLICLY VOICED DISAPPOINTMENT at the verdict and sent both Felt and Miller autographed copies of his latest book, *The Real War*. The former president had inscribed it, "With appreciation for his years of service to the nation. Richard Nixon."

On December 12, the prosecutors dropped the charges against Pat Gray because they said they did not believe they could prove he had authorized the burglaries. Since Gray had not been prosecuted for destroying the evidence taken from Howard Hunt's safe after the Watergate burglary, it meant Gray would go free.

The sentencing of Felt and Miller was set for December 15. That day the *Post* ran an unusual editorial—again, as a reporter, I had nothing to do with it—that took a different tack from the first one. The editorial said that perhaps Felt and Miller were not the ones who should be standing before the judge for sentencing. It posed the question that they might be "the fall guys for a system acquiesced in by countless others and that they themselves did not create."

This editorial closed by saying, "There is nothing to be

gained by sending them to prison. It would be gratuitous and cruel."

I cheered inside.

That day the judge fined Felt $5,000, and Miller $3,500. Neither received a prison sentence.

"I'm now a convicted felon," Felt said outside the courthouse, reminding everyone that it was a "very serious blemish on my whole life."

The D.C. Court of Appeals suspended Felt from practicing law indefinitely.

Soon after the trial, Reagan took office, and a month and a half after the assassination attempt on him by John Hinckley, the new president announced that he had granted full and unconditional pardons to Felt and Miller. In a five-paragraph statement President Reagan said the actions of the two "grew out of their good faith belief that their actions were necessary to preserve the security interests of their country."

He added, "America was at war in 1972, and Messrs. Felt and Miller followed procedures they believed essential to keep the Director of the FBI, the Attorney General, and the President of the United States advised of the activities of hostile foreign powers and their collaborators in this country."

Reagan continued to draw a rather bright ideological line by adding:

"Four years ago thousands of draft evaders and others who violated the Selective Service laws were unconditionally pardoned by my predecessor.

"America was generous to those who refused to serve their country in the Vietnam War. We can be no less generous to two men who acted on high principle to bring an end to the terrorism that was threatening our Nation."

Felt responded publicly in a way that said it all: "I'm so pleased I can hardly contain myself. I don't know how I'm going to thank him."

Nixon sent Felt and Miller each a bottle of champagne with a note that said, "Justice ultimately prevails."

11

I WAS ACUTELY AWARE THAT MY FRIEND HAD DODGED a series of bullets. I backed off. I didn't know the personal side of his ordeal, but I was sure it had exacted a heavy toll.

Around this time, Richard Cohen, a columnist for the *Post* and a good friend of Carl's and mine, came to see me to say that he was pretty sure Deep Throat was Mark Felt. Nora Ephron, Carl's soon to be ex-wife, was on the case and she too was convinced it was Felt, Cohen said. He was going to write a column about this.

I was then the *Post*'s metropolitan editor, and I had nominal supervisory responsibility over Cohen—to the extent that anyone ever could supervise Cohen, one of the smartest, most determined and opinionated writers at the *Post*.

At first I discouraged him from doing the column.

He persisted. It was one of the great mysteries, he said. He recalled how I had passed along a tip to him when he was a Maryland reporter about Vice President Agnew's payoffs before there ever was a formal investigation of Agnew.

Deep Throat was my source, I said, and I have to protect him.

Don't be ridiculous, after so many years? Cohen said. It had been about eight years at that point.

So I misled him, trying as best I could to steer him away from Felt without flat out denying it.

Look, he said, he had heard from someone—Carl or Nora or someone—that at the top of my Deep Throat memos were the initials "M.F."—obviously Mark Felt, right?

It's not him, I said, adopting the well-tested Watergate strategy that when all else fails, lie. I lied, and insisted to Cohen that he had it wrong. W–R–O–N–G! I spelled it out, I recall. A real, safe truth between friends, I indicated, suggesting that I was helping him from writing something monumentally stupid.

Cohen didn't do the column.

I felt bad, but it had been an easy decision. I objected to reporters or columnists trying to figure out the sources used by other reporters. It was cheap, and if everyone did it, no one would have any sources. Our job—the reporters' job collectively—was to protect sources. Even from other reporters.

I also thought I was able to balance the pain. The pain such a column might cause Felt—with the authority of the "M.F." initials—versus my pain as a result of lying to Cohen. If Cohen did the column and really scoped it out, fingered Felt with some supporting evidence, I could imagine all hell breaking loose. Could Reagan take back the pardon? What would Reagan or his administration think upon learning that the new Republican president had just pardoned Deep Throat? Could the new Reagan Justice Department launch a criminal investigation of Felt for talking about FBI information? It had been done before. Could I be called before a grand jury and forced to identify him? If I refused could I be jailed? I knew the answer was probably yes. I started thinking about jail for Felt or me, and I didn't like the idea one bit.

This was one of the easiest lies for me to tell.

Sorry, Richard.

OVER THE YEARS many people have asked me if the identity of Deep Throat would ever be disclosed. I don't remember exactly why or when but sometime back in the 1970s I answered that I thought it should be revealed only after his death, unless in his lifetime he changed his mind and agreed to have it disclosed, an unlikely occurrence I believed.

I thought it should be revealed to set the historical record straight. History should know that a critical source was No.

2 in the FBI. Carl Bernstein and Ben Bradlee seemed to agree, though I don't recall having a serious discussion about this decision with either of them. In many ways, it is a policy question that the *Post* could have addressed. So for decades I said his identity would be revealed after his death. I regularly made the point, only half jokingly, to large audiences I was speaking to, that if you did not know his identity, it was not obvious, but if you did, as I did, it was obvious.

Only two people I knew of questioned this decision. One was the late Lloyd Cutler, the Washington attorney who had been White House counsel to both Presidents Carter and Clinton. Cutler, who died in 2005 at the age of 87, objected that I had publicly identified the late Supreme Court Justice Potter Stewart as a key source for the 1979 book I co-authored on the Supreme Court, *The Brethren.* Cutler maintained that other journalists whom he did not identify believed that a confidential source was forever.

The other objection came from former Nixon lawyer Len Garment. In 2003, after Carl and I sold our Watergate papers to the University of Texas, ensuring that the identities of sources that were still living would be protected, Garment wrote an op-ed piece in *The Wall Street Journal* with the headline "Deep Betrayal." In it he wrote "it is no secret" that he was a source for *The Final Days,* the second Watergate book that Carl and I wrote. Garment had said things in confidence "that I do not believe and did not believe even then."

He never gave a postmortem release, he noted, but realized that history has an interest. He suggested waiting a decent interval of say 20 years after a source's death.

Since then I have encountered no situation in which a confidential source—and I have had dozens of important ones in the administration of President George W. Bush—has raised the possibility of extending the confidentiality beyond death.

I could see the allure some found in trying to establish Deep Throat's identity. It was a mystery that would not go away. Once it was established, it would also mean that dozens if not hundreds of people, once suspects or on lists, had not been the source. Washington is a city that thrives on secrets but simultaneously abhors them, especially someone else's secrets.

One night I ran into Pierre Salinger, who had been press secretary to President Kennedy. We began talking about secret sources. He said that he had never been able to discover the sources for three of the most important, sensational stories of the Kennedy years. The chief suspect for two of the leaks, he said, was President Kennedy himself, but we would never know for sure. I'd give my left one to know, Salinger declared in Kennedy tough-talk form.

In 1982, eight years after publication of *All the President's Men*, John Dean claimed in his book *Lost Honor* that he thought Deep Throat had been Alexander Haig, who had been Kissinger's deputy national security adviser during our Watergate stories. Dean later acknowledged that he was wrong. Others made periodic efforts.

James Mann, a former *Post* colleague and someone who helped me obtain the job at the *Post* in 1971, wrote an article for *The Atlantic Monthly* in May 1992 titled "Deep Throat: An Institutional Analysis." He concluded correctly that Deep Throat had to be someone from the FBI, such as Felt or another official there, because they were trying to keep the White House from politicizing or limiting the Bureau's Watergate investigation.

Mann claimed that during the summer and early fall of 1972 I repeatedly spoke to him or within earshot of "my source at the FBI" or "my friend at the FBI."

I seriously doubt I said this, and I hope I was more careful. I believe I was. After the article appeared, I called Mann, an astute and experienced journalist, then at the *Los Angeles Times,* to complain. I didn't want to sound too high-church about it, but I argued that confidential source discussion within the newsroom should be protected, and in any case it was not for him to decide to reveal alleged details about my source.

In addition, I said that I was certain I did not talk about an FBI source in any form. Even in discussions with Carl, I referred only circumspectly to "my friend." Why would I be more forthright to Mann or within his hearing? Yet he had a reason to say what he did; after all he was right. Mann held his ground but he seemed surprised that I was worried 20 years after the fact. After all, he asked, what was there to protect now? I could hardly explain that the relationship between Deep Throat and me had, how should I say, been sour or bumpy. How could I say I felt emotions ranging from unease to something resembling regret? Mann and I had been friends for more than 20 years, one of those relationships that includes lunch every other year or so. The conversation ended icily, and I don't believe there have been any lunches after that.

One of the most imaginative efforts to determine Deep Throat's identity was undertaken by Fred Weisberger of Turlock, California, for a master's thesis. He sent me a copy of his 109-page paper filled with lists, maps and pictures of my old apartment building. Weisberger had systematically considered 120 possible Deep Throat suspects, including Nixon's nephew (!), Nixon's brother(!!), Nixon's personal secretary, Rose Mary Woods (!!!!). There were names on the list I didn't even recognize—Daniel Davidson and Viron Vaky, supposedly of the NSC staff.

Weisberger then evaluated each on five criteria:

1. A shared past with Woodward.
2. Access to the information.
3. Ability to meet with Woodward.

4.   Personal/professional motive.
5.   Similarities to Deep Throat.

Weisberger concluded that Deep Throat was probably National Security Council staffers Laurence Lynn or Winston Lord. He wrote a strong disclaimer, saying his method was speculative and circumstantial. He also apologized to Lynn and Lord if he was wrong.

Felt made his list of the top 120 suspects but Weisberger incorrectly said that Felt met only one of the five criteria: ability to meet with Woodward. Nonetheless it was a fine effort that included some thoughtful textual analysis of my books and other documents.

IN THE LATE 1990s, Leonard Garment, the Washington lawyer who had been Nixon's former law partner and later his White House counsel and my sometime source (by his own admission) and a renowned conversationalist, called me. This was well before the 2003 op-ed piece he wrote in *The Wall Street Journal* in which he objected to disclosure of sources after their death. He also sent me a letter saying he was undertaking a book to be called *In Search of Deep Throat*. Garment claimed he was determined to solve the mystery of the man and his motive. He asked that we meet. I avoided him and finally told Garment I would not and could not talk about my sources—a principle he knew and understood well. He didn't press.

In 1997 I embarked on a book about the legacy of Watergate and its impact on the modern presidency, from Ford through Clinton. I interviewed many of Felt's former FBI colleagues but I never attempted to contact him, since he had made it clear to me he didn't wish to speak about it. Or it seemed that way. I did try to keep track of him. I learned that he was living with his daughter, Joan, in Santa Rosa, California.

I had continued my newspaper reporting and book writing, never really revisiting Watergate, the Watergate era or its personalities. Occasionally, I would have lunch with John Ehrlichman. Several years after Nixon's resignation and after Ehrlichman had served 18 months in jail, he and I met in Paris, where we were appearing on a French television show. We talked and did a joint interview with *Paris Match*. Afterward, Ehrlichman said he was going to an exhibit of the Impressionist painter Paul Cézanne, and he invited me to go along. Ehrlichman said that for him Watergate was in the past, as forgotten as it could be. He wanted to keep it buried there. If I wanted to deal with him on other matters, we could keep in touch, something short of friendship but more than acquaintances.

At the Cézanne exhibit, he described how he had put his

life back together, and his intention to keep it that way. He had grown a beard, was writing novels, doing some sketching, and living in Santa Fe. Though I guess I could never admire him, I thought he had made the best of his bad situation.

I kept in touch with Dean, who in 1996 came to dinner at our home. Watergate was always hovering in the background with Dean. He was not about to let it go.

In the 18 years between Felt's pardon and 1999, when my book *Shadow: Five Presidents and the Legacy of Watergate* was published, I had made a few halfhearted stabs to contact Felt. But never with much determination, and I never succeeded. I was curious, but my heart wasn't in it. I was no longer the 30-year-old reporter chasing the story but I had naturally become more interested in motive. I knew I eventually had to deal with Felt in some form. There were too many unanswered questions. The historical record was due some answers.

In the summer of 1999 *The Hartford Courant* published a story quoting a 19-year-old named Chase Culeman-Beckman who claimed that Carl's son, Jacob, had told him that Mark Felt was Deep Throat. Culeman-Beckman and Jacob Bernstein had been at a day camp together a decade earlier.

The reporter, David Daley, had contacted Felt in California and quoted Felt as saying, "No, it's not me. I would have done better. I would have been more effective. Deep Throat didn't exactly bring the White House crashing down, did he?"

I read the sentence many times. It was classic Felt, classic Deep Throat. He was, of course, putting himself down. And did Deep Throat bring the White House crashing down? You could answer the question many, many ways, as I had over the years.

12

IF DAVID DALEY OF *THE HARTFORD COURANT* COULD reach Felt, so could I. I stewed and postponed for months, Felt's number on a card near my desk at home. Finally on January 4, 2000, I called the Santa Rosa number and reached him. I felt like a telephone solicitor, not knowing what kind of reception I was going to get. I identified myself and told him that as an old reporter I was going to tape the call. This was perhaps unfriendly, but I wanted a record of what he said. He seemed to recognize my name, but not necessarily me.

"What are you doing?" I asked.

"Well," Felt said in a strong, slow voice, "just trying to get in the time. When you get as old as I am, it gets to be a little bit of a problem."

I asked how old he was.

"Eighty?" he replied. "Let me see, 86 or 87. I'm not sure, I'd have to check. I was born in 1913."

I remarked that my father was born that year also, and said that a key to getting through was to keep active.

"That's one key," Felt replied, "and another key is to realize that getting old has got a lot of problems connected with it. And you just have to put up with them."

"At 56, I find the same thing."

"Believe me," he replied, "you haven't got near the problems that you'll have in another 20 years."

"I'm aware I have that to look forward to," I said.

"It isn't exactly looking forward to it. No, don't look forward to it. Just realize you've got to put up with it."

So far, so good, I thought. Small talk, yes, somewhat odd, but he had not hung up, shouted or voiced displeasure. I was nervous. I knew from my experience with my own father that there was no way to tell his precise mental state, and that memory is problematic. I had written out several lines of questioning that I hoped might elicit the answers I had longed to hear.

"What I wanted to ask you," I began, "if you were to look back on Watergate, not the unraveling of Watergate after the burglary, but prior to the June '72 burglary, and ask the question, 'What was Nixon's undoing?'"

"The trouble is I wouldn't really feel capable of addressing that question," Felt replied. "I have to do a lot of reading and a lot of research and revise and go back and refresh my recollections on a lot of things. . . . It doesn't ring any bell or anything like that."

My stomach sank real low. I asked if he remembered Jack McDermott, who had been head of the FBI's Washington field office in 1973. McDermott once said that after John Ehrlichman had resigned from the White House, several FBI agents were sent to guard his files and office.

"Do you recall that?" I asked.

"No, I don't remember," he said.

"And McDermott said that Nixon came by and pushed one of the agents."

"No, I don't remember that at all," Felt said. "I'm not saying it didn't happen. I'm just saying I don't remember."

I thought it was the perfect answer from someone who was used to being knee-deep in attorneys.

Do you remember when Nixon testified at your trial and Miller's trial? I asked.

"No, I have no recollection of that," Felt answered.

I was surprised. "And eventually when Reagan pardoned you. Does that ring a bell?" That had to dive hard into the memory bank.

"Doesn't ring a bell," Felt said. "No, I don't remember specifically that he pardoned me. I don't remember anything that happened that I would have to be pardoned for. I wasn't convicted."

"Well," I said, "you were convicted and then many years later the Court of Appeals overturned it." It was true, even after the pardon, the next highest court had ordered that the indictment be dismissed—for legal purposes expunging the record.

"I guess that is what I'm thinking about," Felt replied. "Well, no, I don't want to inject myself into it at all, you know, comment on things like that. First place, it happened so long ago. Second place, I don't want to get involved in it any way I don't have to."

That sounded like the man I knew. "Well, you've always wanted to stay out."

"Right," he said.

"Why?" That was the question I desperately wanted answered.

"Well," he said, "just for this reason we're talking about now. There was an awful lot of problems in dealing with the press."

"And the White House," I added.

"Well, I don't really remember any specific problems in dealing with the White House," he said.

I was surprised again.

"I mean I can't recall any specific instances of problem," Felt continued. "I think there must be some record of all that somewhere though. But I can't comment on it."

"Sure," I said. "What are you spending your time doing?"

"This afternoon I'm just spending my time putting in time waiting until it gets late enough for me to eat my dinner."

I was relieved, terribly relieved, that at least on the surface he was friendly.

"And that's not easy to do," he continued.

"Where do you live exactly?" I asked. "You live with your daughter?"

"Yes," he said. "She's working, she's a teacher, and so she's busy all the time. I just try to stay in the background, stay out of her way. She's got three fine boys. I try to deal with them the best way I can. All is going well though from that standpoint."

I said that I had gone back and reviewed some of the Watergate files from the FBI and had found the memo he had written about an article Carl and I had published in the *Post* about Howard Hunt visiting the ITT lobbyist Dita Beard.

"I remember the name Howard Hunt," Felt said. "I don't remember the other one, Beard?"

"She was the woman who wrote the ITT memo."

"I don't remember that at all. Yeah, one of the problems being as old as I am is you don't remember well. I'm sure something that would have been sharp and clear 20 years ago is real fuzzy and hazy today. You'll find out."

He then asked, "How old are you?"

"As I said, 56."

"Well, you're just getting at the threshold of life," he said.

I laughed. "I wish I could persuade you to remember and talk more."

"Well," he began. There was a long, long silence. "No, I can't," he said. Then as if the phone connection had been broken, he said, "Hello?"

It was an old trick, I recalled. If you are in a phone conversation you don't want to have, pretend there is a bad connection. But it is possible, or even more than likely that there had been some disruption or he had thought there was. "Yes? Sir?" I said.

There was another long silence, but the connection was clearly intact.

Then Felt said something odd. "Let's just, I'll hang up," he said firmly and conclusively, then added, "And this closet door can be a closed door."

That was the Mark Felt I had known. He was terminating the conversation. Period. I knew the brush-off well.

"Okay," I said. "Good talking to you."

"Well, it's good talking to you," he said, sounding sincere.

"Hope all is well."

"Okay," he said.

"Bye."

"Bye," he replied, hanging up, closing the closet door once more.

My mind was racing. On one level, I was happy. Felt's anger and bitterness at the world, the FBI, Nixon or me seemed to have dissipated. But so had his memory. There were traces of his old self and personality—intimations of Deep Throat. What should I do?

I WAS SCHEDULED to give a speech at the University of California at Davis at the end of the next month, Sunday night, February 27. I arranged to hire a black Lincoln Town Car and driver to take me the next day on the two-hour trip from Davis to Santa Rosa, a beautiful region north of the Napa and Sonoma wine country. Felt lived on a street called Redford Place—an irony not lost on me.

The driver had a street map of Santa Rosa. I drew a map for myself on the back of a four-by-six card and asked to be left off at Northwest Community Park. I didn't want the driver to know where I was going. I told him I wanted to walk to my destination since it was such a nice day and asked him to wait at the park no matter how long. It would be at least several hours, perhaps, I hoped, much longer. Once again I was playing by Felt's old counterintelligence rules.

It was about a 10-block walk to the house, a nice, basic split-level California suburban home dominated by a large two-car garage. I rang the doorbell and a woman finally answered. It was Felt's daughter, Joan. I introduced myself, and said I was down at UC Davis and had some time and wanted to see her father.

Joan Felt, my age, is a slender, pleasant-looking woman

with short hair. She teaches Spanish at two of the local colleges. She was very welcoming, and shouted down from the kitchen to the garage, which had been converted into an apartment for her father.

Dad, there is someone here to see you—Bob Woodward from *The Washington Post.*

Felt came up the steps. He was in remarkable physical shape, not overweight, only a little stiff in his walk, his posture erect as it had always been. He smiled, his mouth lifting more on the left side of his face with the ironic twist that I remembered so well. He took my hand, and I his. I looked into his eyes through my eyeglasses and his eyeglasses. I could sense recognition but it didn't seem personal. It had been nearly two decades. He was dressed casually and still had his full helmet of white-gray hair. He and Joan were going grocery shopping before she went off to teach a class, and he was thinking about his lunch.

"Can we pick up a dish on the way home?" he asked her.

"Well," I said, jumping in, "I'll take you out and we'll get some lunch."

"You will?" Joan said with mild surprise.

I explained I had a car down the road, and we could go to his favorite restaurant.

"Okay," Felt said.

I was elated. We were going to be alone for the first time in decades.

We went out to get in Joan's van, and Felt explained that he was kind of slow getting around. "It's a real pleasure," he said, looking at me.

We got in the van, Joan driving, Mark in the front seat. I was in the back.

"It's too bad that my memory isn't better," Mark volunteered, "because I would certainly end up with a very favorable impression of Bob Woodward and his work at the *Post*."

I was astonished. I wanted to jump in the front seat and hug him. Maybe, I thought, we would finally get all of this out in the open, but I didn't want to do it in front of his daughter. "You remember it?" I asked, referring to my work at the *Post* and his contribution.

"I have to be reminded," he said. "What's the reason you're here now?"

"I just wanted to chat with you and see how you were. I called you last month."

"I don't remember," he said.

"Are you still hot on the trail of Deep Throat?" Joan asked.

I laughed nervously. I couldn't see the expression on his face. "I don't have to get on the trail," I said.

"Bob has always done a very outstanding job as a reporter," Mark said.

I was almost bouncing in the back seat. Now we were getting somewhere!

Joan said that her mother, Audrey, had died some 15

years ago, and they had lived in California for 10 years. She asked how her dad and I had met.

Did she know? I wondered.

"I'm sure we became acquainted with each other during what would you call those days?" Mark Felt said.

"The Nixon Watergate days," I replied.

We arrived at the grocery store in a nearby mall, and got out of the van. I reminded Mark that he was the same age as my father. "Same age as you," I said. "Eighty-six."

"Yeah," Joan said.

"Am I 86?"

"Yes," she said.

"I knew I was in my 80s."

I gave a big laugh.

We entered the grocery store and wheeled the cart around the aisles.

A shopper recognized me from some television appearance and asked if I hadn't written some exposé book at one time.

I nodded. Mark seemed oblivious. I asked him what books he had been reading because he had always loved books.

"Joan," he said, "I can't remember those two authors I was so intrigued with?"

"Danielle Steel," she said.

I was surprised that he was reading lowbrow stuff.

"Are you familiar with Steel?" he asked me.

I nodded.

"Of course," Felt said. "I enjoyed those books very much."

"Do you read Tom Clancy at all?" I asked.

"I don't believe I have," Mark Felt said.

"Dad, you have read him."

"Well, a lot of things I don't remember," he said, turning to me. "In Washington," he asked, "your situation is pretty much the same?"

I nodded yes.

"How many books have you written?"

I said nine.

"Well, that's a good start," he said.

We went through the checkout counter.

"I'm sure glad you stopped by," he said to me.

"Can I take him to lunch?" I asked Joan.

"If you keep him fat-free," she cautioned.

Joan gave me directions to a good restaurant. "They have healthy food there. One glass of wine, no more."

I promised, took an oath, pledged.

"Here's what Dad likes for lunch," she said, mentioning something about a special glazed or grazed tofu dish.

I didn't believe it was his favorite. I hate tofu. But tofu it would be.

"He went on a 100 percent raw diet for two months and brought his cholesterol down," Joan said proudly.

As we drove back I asked Mark if he remembered Ed Miller.

"I remember Ed Miller very well," he replied.

"When the article came out in *Time* magazine about Dad possibly being Deep Throat, he became quite a local celebrity for a while," Joan said, explaining that his doctor had been pleased. *Time* had done several articles over the years, running lists of possible Deep Throats.

"The only problem I'm encountering is a loss of memory," Mark said. "I'll remember this visit of yours, Bob."

"You're more relaxed too," I said, recalling the memorably tense meetings we had.

"Yeah, I think so."

"I don't remember what you were like when you were still working for the FBI," Joan said.

"What was I like?" Mark asked.

"What was he like?" she echoed.

Father and daughter were asking me what he was like. I was still thinking paranoid thoughts. Seeing him, talking to him brought back all that sense of mystery, danger and the unknowable. So I punted, saying he was very efficient, worked hard and lived under lots of stress.

"Did he seem stressed?" Joan asked.

I said yes. Her father had been so tightly wound then that his springs could have exploded.

"You don't remember, Joan?" I asked. "What were you doing then?"

"Living my life independently," she answered.

"How old are you now?" Mark asked again.

"Fifty-six," I answered.

We arrived back at their house, and Mark went back to his garage apartment to change and put on a coat for lunch. I went into the kitchen with Joan.

"The doctor says he has dementia," she explained, a loss of mental power and memory. But he was not afflicted with Alzheimer's disease. He has had a heart condition and a shunt had been placed in his heart. The raw diet had got his cholesterol down from 250 to 125, a remarkable drop, she said. She obviously loved him and was taking extraordinary care of him. Only one glass of wine, or one martini at lunch, she ordered, almost wagging her finger at me.

I left to get the driver and car. I was chuckling and whistling as I walked the 10 blocks back to the park where the driver was waiting. I was exhilarated. It was as if some pall was beginning to lift.

When I returned, Mark had changed and was clearly delighted to get out of the house. I introduced him just as Mark to the driver, who took us to the Stony Point Bar and Grill. We sat in a small booth. He had fish and a glass of wine. I decided not to turn my tape recorder on.

It was a difficult lunch. Mark knew we had met, that we

had talked, probably a good number of times, perhaps many times. He could recall nothing about the flowerpot, nothing about my marked *New York Times,* nothing about the Rosslyn underground parking garage. Did he recall being my source, the one that was called Deep Throat?

He said he didn't know.

Had he read *All the President's Men?* Seen the movie? Did he recognize his role, what he had done, how he had helped us, taken supreme risks to his career, put everything in jeopardy?

He didn't remember, he said, carefully noting that that didn't mean it hadn't happened.

Maybe it was the wine, maybe he didn't remember, maybe he didn't wish to remember. Maybe the denial was so embedded in his persona, his way of life, that he couldn't or didn't want to unlock it.

I paid for lunch, $47.25, including tip.

The driver took us back to the Felt house, and I asked him to wait. I was going inside and had no idea when I would be back.

Mark and I went to his garage apartment. It was sparely furnished. He had a television, books, a narrow bed. A couple of chairs filled out the room. I took out my tape recorder and explained that I wanted to get his recollections. This was an interview for the record, for history.

13

THE OLD TIMES," I BEGAN.

"But I don't remember," he said.

"I can understand you don't remember. You remember the Nixon period a little bit?"

"Vaguely," he replied, "but I still don't have any specific recollections from it."

"Do you remember when you met him, when you met Nixon?"

"I can't remember. I met him but I can't remember when it was."

"And kind of your attitude toward him?" I asked. "Because you were always suspicious, you always knew there were funny things going on."

Mark gave two deep, very wise, knowing chuckles. "Well, I maybe conveyed that impression to a lot of people."

BOB WOODWARD

"Including—" I began. I was going to say me.

"Part of it was my assignment, you know working for the FBI," he interjected.

"Do you remember what first made you suspicious? You know the wiretaps going on?"

"I remember some," he said. "I don't remember that was any particular cause of concern to me," he added.

"The Pentagon Papers," I asked.

"Yeah, they were enough to make you a little suspicious."

"Whether there was some event or something that stuck in your mind that there is funny stuff going on?"

"No," he said, "I don't have any specifics like that."

"Was it Ehrlichman? Remember Ehrlichman?" I asked. Ehrlichman had been the nemesis, the embodiment of White House pressure.

"I remember Ehrlichman," Felt said. "I don't remember any specific dealings with him."

"Do you remember when you and I met?"

He was blank, his eyes sincere.

"At all?"

"No. No. I don't."

"Remember back in those years when we met and chatted?" I asked. Over lunch I had recalled for him the evening we had met at the White House.

"I remember the area and a time but I don't remember specifically anything."

176

"I was in the Navy," I said and was at the White House delivering papers. "You came over there for something and I don't remember what it was."

"I wouldn't know either," he said.

"And you were very nice to me like you were today."

"Well, that's good," he said. "I think that's just part of my personality, but I don't think I was putting on anything just especially for you."

"Yes, but you were willing to help and take some chances."

"I'm glad," he said.

"You remember the reasons for that or the impulse for that?" I asked. This was my question: Why?

"No, I don't remember that background at all."

"Because at some risk to yourself, because the FBI was investigating Watergate and you knew the clamps were on pretty hard," I said.

"Yeah, that's true."

"You were kind of saying, there's more here and I was nagging you pretty hard. I was pretty young."

"I don't remember," he replied. Again, his eyes seemed sincere.

"You don't remember at all," I said. Certainly, I thought he would remember the big events—the biggest of all. "And remember when Nixon resigned?"

"Well, I do just vaguely remember. I'd have to be reminded with specific examples of things that came up."

"Do you remember why he had to resign?"

"I don't remember that at all," he replied in an even voice.

He had forgotten the main event, or the reason for the main event—the Watergate cover-up which he had watched unfold for nearly a year, right before his eyes, day by day, interview by interview, White House concealment upon White House concealment. "Do you remember why you left the Bureau? Do you remember why you retired?"

"I think I left the Bureau only for the reason that it was . . ." he said. "I had served my length of time and I was eligible for retirement and I wanted to go to college, wanted to go to law school. So I think those were the reasons."

He had gone to law school in the 1930s, before he'd joined the Bureau. Being a lawyer was certainly part of his core identity. "To go to law school after the Bureau?" I asked, gently I hope.

"I don't remember."

"You don't have to," I said. This was turning into an inquisition, the last thing I had in mind.

"Well, that's good," he said.

"Do you remember my friendly face?" I asked.

"Yes."

"Always nagging and carping?"

He neither agreed nor disagreed.

"Do you think what Carl Bernstein and I did was right?"

"Yes," he said. "I do think what you did was right."

"Why was it so hard?"

"A lot of people in there motivating one way or the other, some opposing you, some favoring you," he said. "There was just a complicated situation. People were just trying to . . . help out different groups."

I wanted to go back to the why. "Was it because you knew me that you were willing to help or that you just felt it smelled?"

"No, it wasn't because I knew you, I'm sure," he replied.

"It was because I was a nag," I said.

"Yeah."

"And then you got mad about it, you thought we went too far. There are some memos—"

"Are there some memos to that effect?"

It was my turn to say, "Yeah."

"Well, I've forgotten those," he said.

"You were saying, oh well, Woodward and Bernstein, sometimes it's half fiction or there's a lot of fiction," I said, referring specifically to his memo about the Dita Beard story.

"I don't remember writing that at all," he said.

"But then saying they are clearly getting information out of the FBI or the Justice Department."

"I have very little recollection of that period," he said.

"Was that kind of to cover yourself because people in the Bureau were mad we were writing these stories?"

"No, I don't think so," he replied. "I think because of the level where I was, I could have done anything I wanted so far as Bureau policy was concerned."

"Well, Gray was kind of running the show, wasn't he?" I asked.

"He was after he got his clues from me."

"Yeah, what were the clues?"

"I don't remember specifically. I mean I was the one who was on top, making final decisions."

Was it possible, I wondered, that somehow being Deep Throat and talking to me was Bureau policy, a final decision he had made? But I didn't ask. "You knew the most and you saw there was much more to it, the overall. That there was a big—"

"Well, I guess so," he said. "I don't remember now specifically."

"You did more than guess," I said. "A lot of things came across your desk."

"Oh, yeah."

"Did they ever keep anything from you, do you think?"

"No. I don't think so. When you say they, I don't know who that would be."

"People in the FBI," I said. His mind was still functioning,

I thought. The lawyer's question about who "they" would be was par for the course.

"There is nothing they would hold back," he said confidently.

"Remember that Pat Gray destroyed some of the evidence that John Dean gave him?" Certainly that was one of the very big Watergate stories. As was the demise of Gray.

"I don't remember that, no."

"And Gray really left in disgrace," I said.

"I guess so. I don't really remember about that either."

"They brought Ruckelshaus in."

"I remember Ruckelshaus."

"You weren't wild about that," I noted.

"No."

"And then you retired. They could have given you the job because you were effectively the No. 2, weren't you?"

"Yes, I think I was," he said.

"Were you unhappy when you had to leave?"

"It was time."

"Remember when they went after Ed Miller and you for those break-ins on the Weathermen?"

"I don't remember anything specifically."

"You had to go on trial? Remember that?" I wanted to try this again, but I did not want to lead the witness, though I knew I already was.

"No."

"And they convicted you and then Reagan pardoned you?"

"Well, that rings a bell, yeah."

"That must have felt good?"

"Well, I'm sure it did."

"Remember Jack McDermott?" I asked. He had been the special agent in charge of the Washington field office doing the Watergate investigation.

"The name sounds familiar but I don't remember anything other than that."

"What else should I know?" I asked him. That is the reporter's final desperate question. I didn't want a recording of him not recalling he was Deep Throat, or worse, denying it.

"Well, what I was thinking," he said. "This is all vague in my recollection. Why don't you be thinking about it a little bit this afternoon and later on and maybe you could write out specific questions that you wanted to ask."

"Any papers, files, notes?" I asked. It was a reporter's other last, somewhat desperate question.

"No. Nothing at all."

"Remember what your book was called?"

"*The FBI Pyramid*," he replied immediately and correctly. "Well, I think that's about it for today. I certainly thank you for the company and the excellent lunch. I'll be available here."

I shut off the tape recorder and asked some more questions. His answers got me nowhere. But I wanted to salvage something, at least some of the feeling of goodwill. I turned the tape recorder back on.

"What's nice is you feel friendly about it now," I said. "You were unhappy with me for a long time."

"I can understand that. I'm sure I was."

"Good to see the air cleared," I said optimistically.

"Good," he said.

I left in a tangle of emotions. I did not want to become confrontational or accusatory or reckless. I hoped I had not stepped over that line. But there were still those ultimate questions, the ones I could not bring myself to ask or had not asked 28 years earlier, and that I could not seem to reach now: Why were you Deep Throat? What was your motive? Who are you? Who were you?

Worse, I had to consider whether the man I had dealt with in this visit was the same man I had made the pledge of confidentiality to. What was my responsibility? To whom? I went home to Washington.

As I replayed the visit in my mind and made a transcript of our conversation, I realized I had one strong feeling toward Mark Felt. And that feeling was gratitude. He not only had helped me on Watergate. He had showed me the way to develop relationships of trust for my reporting.

OVER THE MONTHS and several years that followed, as I debated with myself and my wife about what to do about possible disclosure of Felt's identity should he die, I knew I was bumping up against some serious practical questions.

Repeatedly, those I had interviewed for my books or stories for the *Post* had cited my willingness to protect a source such as Deep Throat for nearly 30 years as a reason they were willing to talk about some of the most sensitive and Top Secret deliberations in the U.S. government. "You'll protect sources," was a common refrain, often delivered with a knowing chuckle or a direct or indirect reference to Deep Throat.

I would even say at times that this was a "Deep Throat" conversation, and some of those in the most sensitive positions or best-placed crossroads of the American government would nod and then talk in remarkable detail, plowing through security classifications and other barriers as if they did not exist, including private conversations with a president. Deep Throat, or the concept of rigid source protection, became the unstated part of the conversation. The intimate and important struggles of government, the conflict and lethal bureaucratic maneuver warfare, had become the Washington story as much as scandal. Source protection was as important on these matters as on crime and national security. I had been able to write books about the inside of the Supreme Court, the Hollywood drug culture, the CIA, the Pentagon, the Clinton White House, and later about the administration of President George W. Bush, the 9/11 terrorist attacks and the Iraq war. The FBI, the CIA and the secrets of National Security Council deliberations were often cornerstones of this reporting.

Reporting for a newspaper or a book is in part a matter of efficiency—getting to the heart of a matter quickly, finding those who know or have documents, and building a relationship of trust with them as quickly as possible.

The Deep Throat legacy was a foundation of establishing the compact: I would never tell. Often during the first interviews, subjects would start talking almost at once. In an odd way, many, or certainly some, wanted to deliver the goods, the secrets. The transaction with the reporter was important, not only for the reporter but also for them.

I did not want to do anything to jeopardize this legacy or advantage. The opportunities for the future were more important than disclosing Deep Throat's identity.

It is critical that confidential sources feel they would be protected for life. There needed to be a model out there where people could come forward or speak when contacted, knowing they would be protected. It was a matter of my work, a matter of honor. Mark Felt was entitled to the promise of anonymity in his lifetime. After his death, which I realized could come at any time, the story could be told. His family, friends and former FBI colleagues could be made to understand, I hoped. Only a full rendering of all I knew would make this possible.

But the Felt of the 1970s no longer existed. Unless there were some secret record he had kept or had told to someone unknown to me, the answers to the main questions were already unavailable. These questions, including everything from the technical, wiring-diagram issues of observing the flowerpot and getting to my copy of *The New York Times,* to the all-important question of his motive, were still not fully answered. What psychological strategies of self-justification did he have? Did he need them?

I owed Felt a great deal, and I wanted to be careful. Like Ben Bradlee, the editor of the *Post,* Mark Felt had in some respects been an extra father.

Setting and filling out the historical record was insufficient reason to disclose his identity. But his identity was crucial to a full understanding of Watergate. Mark Felt is the companion piece to the Nixon tapes.

While the tapes prove that Nixon regularly ordered criminal action and abused government power, Mark Felt is important less for his name than for the position he held as No. 2 in the FBI. The system of justice had been so polluted and corrupted and politicized by Nixon and his men that the FBI could never get to the bottom of Watergate. The law and the rules had been set aside and subverted. Mark Felt was driven to expose what was going on. He had to do it his way. But without him, and, it must be said, without countless others who talked as confidential sources and the prosecutors and Judge Sirica and the Senate and House, you never would or could have gotten to the Nixon tapes. The tapes are the inner Watergate story.

Felt risked much in talking to me. I had never fully assessed his risk. I wonder if he had. That would likely remain another unanswered question. But when Felt told *The Hartford Courant* reporter in 1999, "I would have done better. I would have been more effective," I wonder if part of him knew that, given the stakes, he might not have risked enough. He was careful and protective of himself—remarkably so. Or perhaps he calibrated it just right. He got the story out without exposing himself.

14

___

THE FBI AGENTS WORKING THE INITIAL WATERGATE
investigation in 1972 knew many of the top Nixon people were lying. Bob Lill, an agent from 1966 to 1988, was effectively the deputy working the Watergate case in 1972. In
1998, I interviewed Lill, who recalled the time he and another agent interviewed John Mitchell in 1972. "Mitchell
just said," Lill recalled, "big smile, 'I don't know anything,
just what I read in the papers. What do you want from me?'"

Lill said the 10-minute interview was almost comic. "We
laughed about it." He added, "We thought everybody was
lying in the beginning. I mean it was just kind of, we just
took it for granted."

When the CIA tried to halt the FBI investigation, Lill
said, the FBI agents on the case were going to refuse. "A

Teletype went back saying, if we are prevented from following these leads as a group we would consider resigning." In all there were 15 to 20 agents who felt this way. "There was certainly a unanimity among us that we can't back off. This is ridiculous. This smacks of a cover-up in itself, and we've got to pursue this. Let them know in no uncertain terms we're all together on this.

"What we were up against," Lill said, "—an attempt to thwart the whole thing, but I think that it should be known that the integrity of the agents was, you can't do this. We know it's too important. We know this is too significant an avenue of investigation. You just can't stop it and this request from CIA is hollow."

Nixon resigned in 1974 after the so-called smoking gun tapes were disclosed showing that on June 23, 1972, he asked the CIA to stop the FBI Watergate investigation on bogus national security grounds. Part of John Mitchell's conviction in the Watergate cover-up trial in 1975 was based on his lying to FBI agents Lill and Daniel C. Mahan.

It's pretty clear that Mark Felt knew about the discontent and suspicions of the field agents in 1972. So there was more to his knowledge than the written record in FBI files. The atmosphere around the FBI and the attitude of the agents shouted one message: The Nixon men are lying and the White House is covering up.

• • •

FOR THE BETTER PART OF 2000 I continued to sit on the Deep Throat dilemma. The only person I discussed this with was my wife, Elsa Walsh. I had told her the identity of Deep Throat in the early 1980s, years before we were married. I told her because Deep Throat was a big part of my past. Elsa and I discussed such questions as, What would be right? What would Mark Felt really want now? What would be journalistically proper? What would be safe, for both Felt and for me—and for the *Post* and journalism? At times, Elsa said she thought it might be best to take the secret to my grave.

Clearly, nothing should be done until Felt released me from the agreement. It had to be freely given. But the man who had made the agreement, who had set the strictest terms of confidentiality in 1972, was not accessible to me, or to anyone. Could an 86-year-old man suffering from dementia or what appeared to be severe memory loss decide what was in his best interests? What were his interests? I could not even get at what he might be afraid of if indeed he was afraid of anything. On my visit in 2000 he had treated me as a friend. He had not been fearful. His daughter, Joan, had told others it was as if her father and I were celebrating. Her suspicions were greatly intensifying, but he apparently continued to deny to her that he had been Deep Throat.

Later in 2000, Leonard Garment, the former White House counsel during the later phases of Watergate, published his book, *In Search of Deep Throat: The Greatest Political*

Mystery of Our Time. Garment insisted that John Sears, a former Nixon staffer who had left the White House before Watergate, had been Deep Throat. He was obviously mistaken, and I said so publicly. Sears heatedly denied it, unsure whether he was being flattered or libeled. Which, of course, was always one of the questions about the real Deep Throat. But in his book, Garment, who later seemed to accept that he got it wrong, made some important observations.

Garment had believed he could analyze his way into the answer, think it through, use his mind to find the solution. He is an analyst, not an investigator. As he sorted through possible candidates, he noted that Felt had knowledge and motive. "The trouble with Felt's candidacy was that Deep Throat in *All the President's Men* simply did not sound to me like a career FBI man," Garment wrote. On that basis and perhaps that basis alone, Garment struck Felt from his list of suspects. There is no evidence in Garment's book that he ever tried to track down Felt, review the FBI files on Watergate, or read Felt's book, *The FBI Pyramid.*

As Garment wrote, "Deep Throat's unique contribution was to talk with Woodward about Nixon's White House. Deep Throat knew about the clockwork craziness in that place. He knew the sound of Nixon angry; he knew things about the character of the various people involved in the cover-up."

Felt's book reveals that he thought he knew the angry Nixon personally when he spoke with the president after the 1972 assassination attempt on Governor George Wallace about Arthur Bremer. Nixon's "Well, it's too bad they didn't really rough up the son of a bitch!" is a classic, though the tape shows Nixon more subdued. Felt's recounting of the efforts of John Dean and John Ehrlichman to pressure the FBI pretty well establishes that he knew the character of some of those involved in the Watergate cover-up.

Garment focused on Deep Throat's mind and temperament, but not all FBI men are alike. Some agents are well defended within their official persona and play to the stereotype—buttoned-down, tight and by-the-book. That does not mean that is who they are. Understanding concealment is part of the spy hunter's art.

But in analyzing the stories that Carl and I published in the *Post* and our narrative about our reporting in *All the President's Men*, especially the details of the Deep Throat conversations, Garment landed on the significance of what Deep Throat had to say. Garment also understood the importance of the October 10, 1972, story when we wrote that Watergate was not just an isolated event but was part of a broader, massive campaign of political spying and sabotage.

Garment recounts the Deep Throat meeting before Carl and I wrote that story. "Even though Deep Throat succeeded, in this lengthy meeting, in not delivering up very much in the way of specific information," he wrote, "he gave Woodward and Bernstein what they needed: an organizing principle." The story and its narrative of the activities of Segretti and others "stands as a remarkable piece of journalism. . . . Woodward and Bernstein had, in a general way and with the help of Deep Throat, figured out Watergate by October of 1972."

That story, as Garment noted, began, "FBI agents have established . . ." "FBI" was also in the headline.

Someone with a more investigative bent might have been curious about the FBI, its agents and files.

AT THE END OF APRIL 2002, there was a call on my voice mail at the *Post* from someone who identified himself as Mark Felt Jr. He left a number for me to call. I waited several days, hoping to suggest that I attached no urgency to the matter, whatever it was. I knew Mark had a son who was his namesake. I fretted for several days and then phoned Mark Jr., a 55-year-old American Airlines pilot who lives in Florida. We talked on April 30, 2002.

Mark Jr. had a stunning message about his dad. "He has told us for the first time in all these years that he was Deep Throat." First, the elder Mark Felt had told this to his caregiver, and then told Joan and Mark Jr. The elder Felt's former longtime girlfriend, a woman named Yvette, had called Joan to say that in the 1980s, Mark Sr. had told her he had been Deep Throat. Yvette said he claimed that she was the only person he had ever told and had pledged her to keep the secret.

"The whole thing has come as a big surprise," Felt Jr. said.

I said that because so many possible Deep Throat candidates had died or been eliminated, I was no longer going to comment on the matter. Period. I said I would call Joan.

The family had brought a lawyer in to represent their interests, John D. O'Connor, a former assistant U.S. attorney and litigation specialist in San Francisco.

I talked by phone with O'Connor on May 6 and May 9. He said he had recently met with Mark Felt Sr. "He admitted to me he was Deep Throat," O'Connor said.

I nearly gasped. There it was. Finally out.

"He is waffling now about whether he wants it to come out," O'Connor continued. Felt was worried about what the FBI agents—apparently past and present—might think of him.

It was the old question: Was Felt patriot or traitor?

I reached Joan on May 10. She first mentioned her father's condition. He had fallen and broken a hip, she said, and he had had another stroke. And, she added, her dad was not sure of the right course. He was worried about the security of the family, and said disclosure might "dishonor the family" and he did not want to do that.

"He goes in and out of lucidity," she said, but he was obviously and profoundly troubled. He was up all night after they discussed the issue of Deep Throat.

She was going to put him on the phone but she wanted me to know that her dad had been taken on a long drive that day and had come back very tired.

Mark came to the phone and I identified myself. "How are you?" I asked.

"Well, I'm okay," he said in a direct, cheerful voice. "How are you?"

He wondered how I had come down there, but I said I was in D.C.

"I'm in D.C. too, wherever Joan's house is. I guess it's not D.C.," he said. His voice was clear.

I reminded him that he was in Santa Rosa, California. I said I had a question: "Whether you can crank your mind back 30 years ago and so forth during the Watergate period and whether you remember me, and whether you remember helping me?"

"Well," he said, "I can remember pretty much but I tend to, I'm very forgetful and I tend to forget things now."

"Do you remember helping because you were very important?"

"No, I don't remember."

Any recollection of that period at all? I asked.

"No," he replied sadly.

When you were working in the Bureau?

"No, I don't have any recollection. Many things are completely gone."

Did he recall 1974 when Nixon resigned?

"No."

Do you remember Pat Gray?

"Well, yes and no."

What do you remember about him?

"I don't remember anything about him," Felt replied.

After Hoover died, he became acting director of the FBI, I reminded him.

"No," he said. "I don't remember that."

Do you have any recollection of Nixon trying to push the FBI around?

"No."

Do you remember when you and I met in the White House? I recalled for him that I was then in the Navy and he had come to see someone, perhaps Haig, in 1970.

"No, I don't remember that."

I don't want to push your memory any more than it's there, I said.

He seemed to appreciate that. No doubt he spent a good deal of time explaining and apologizing for his faulty memory.

You and I were friends, I said.

"That's right," he replied, perking up.

You were a stand-up guy, I said. "You know what I mean by that?"

"I'm proud that you use it," he said.

What could I say? I was touched, and I felt an urge to cry out or just cry. I said goodbye, and he hung up.

I was trying to bring him in, establish his authentic memory. What an elusive notion—authentic memory. What did that mean? In 1992, Iran-contra Independent Counsel Lawrence Walsh had insisted on taking a sworn deposition from former President Ronald Reagan more than three years after Reagan had left office. Reagan was only 81 then but clearly in mental decline. I had obtained a copy of the transcript for my book *Shadow: Five Presidents and the Legacy of Watergate*. It was painful reading. Reagan couldn't recall if George Shultz had been his secretary of state or Ed Meese his counselor, both of whom were among his longtime friends and associates. Reagan was read portions of his own diary, and he said something I'll never forget: "It's like I wasn't president at all."

Very sad. As I reflected about this I was sure that I didn't want to badger Mark Felt in the same manner. I didn't want Felt to have to say, in effect, "It's like I wasn't Deep Throat at all."

I was conscious of the extent to which I was imposing my point of view on him. To me, being Deep Throat was his most important role in life. To history, it would certainly be. But was it to him? Or was it the 31 years of service to the FBI? Or his years as one of Hoover's men, or the last year of Hoover's life as the director's right-hand man? Or was it something else? Without being melodramatic, was there some stray Rosebud in his past?

There was my version of Felt—restrained, careful but really gutsy and courageous. He had walked the road and played the part of secret informer so well. Surely that would be history's version. Right? He had carved out his role and found a way to serve a higher principle. Right?

But what of the version he had of himself? I would never know. Who did he owe allegiance to as he defined it? At one time long ago he was obviously torn, perhaps ripped up inside more than I or anyone could have imagined or known. Like many people, he had played two roles. That was it. Inevitably he was both. And the two might not fit together neatly at all. Was that the paradox of personality?

I immediately called Joan to explain that I believed her father had little or no valid memory—nothing that could really be trusted.

Joan said that in the last week he had recalled Pat Gray. Maybe this was a bad day and he was tired, she said. The early afternoons were generally when he was best.

"He always remembers you," she said. "It's amazing he remembers you actually. He doesn't usually remember people he didn't know quite well." She paused briefly. "Maybe he knew you better than I thought."

15

In the spring of 2002, I asked Ben Bradlee to come to my home to read the first draft of my telling of the Deep Throat story. He spent the better part of the day, Thursday, May 30, reading, making a few suggestions. In the end he said it was consistent with his memory—at least the portions of which he had firsthand knowledge, and what I had told him decades ago. In most ways he seemed pleased that I had committed the story to paper, that it proved once and for all that there was a Deep Throat, and that he was a single individual.

Over sandwiches in the sunroom, Bradlee said he had one overriding question, and he posed it with the verbal, facial and body conviction and emphasis that it seems only he can muster. It is Bradlee as Robards accurately portrayed him. When Ben speaks this way, it gets your attention. It is theatrical but genuine; he shares his conclusion as if all his life experience and knowledge is being brought to this very moment. The intimacy is almost overwhelming.

"You've got one problem, pal," Bradlee said. "Do you owe allegiance to a man who is no longer that man who you knew and gave your word to?"

He let me hang on the question for a moment—a question I had already considered, the one I was weighing.

"The answer is yes—an unequivocal YES," Bradlee said, answering his own question. You have to be true to the deal, the agreement and the relationship that existed back in the early 1970s, he said. The 88-year-old Mark Felt is just not the same person, he said. Felt's successor self, if you will, is the victim of frailty and memory loss. The "sound mind" provision of a last will and testament addresses this, he said, and Felt doesn't pass the test.

It underscored the problem of establishing Felt's "real wishes." Bradlee also noted that I might get Felt to acknowledge he was Deep Throat once, but perhaps he wouldn't say it twice. If I was seriously considering doing anything before Felt died, Bradlee recommended, Don't.

I NEXT CALLED MY LAWYER, Robert Barnett of the law firm of Williams & Connolly. Bob, a counselor and friend, has negotiated my book deals for two decades. A law clerk to Supreme Court Justice Byron White in the early 1970s, Bob has an unusual bipartisan practice, acting as agent for Republicans such as former Secretary of State George Shultz, former Vice President Dan Quayle, Vice President Dick Cheney's wife, Lynne, and Democrats, including former President Bill Clinton and his wife, Senator Hillary Rodham Clinton.

Barnett did not need to know the identity of Deep Throat, and I didn't tell him. I said the person, who was now very elderly, seemed to be on the verge of agreeing that his identity could or should be released publicly. Should that story be told before his death? And if so, how? I asked him to think about the issue comprehensively.

When Bob is asked to address an issue, he surrounds it. Given his years navigating the shoals of Washington politics, he sees angles that I would not imagine. When he is your lawyer, he devotes himself entirely to your interest. He has a framework for analyzing any problem: Everyone else has real or potential interests other than yours. His job is to identify your interests and yours alone. I wanted him to contemplate the question because I knew his mind would be circling around and around the issues during his nonbillable, off-duty hours. That way I would not only be getting the very best legal and overall advice, I would be getting a genuine bargain. He doesn't charge for the hours he is thinking in the shower or on an airplane. Or tossing in his sleep. Thank God.

Barnett came to Sunday night dinner on June 2. Dressed casually, he bounded in. He is average in build with large glasses and thinning hair. Everything about him is quick, rapid-fire—his movements, his speech. He is edgy and focused. Those who don't know him might, at first, think he is nervous. Since he charges more than $12 a minute, it might be his way of saying you have his undivided attention. He brought with him the homework he had done, several copies of a single sheet of paper headed "ISSUES TO BE CONSIDERED." It included everything—a possible book, magazine excerpts, movie rights and the interests of *The Washington Post.*

Given the frail state of Deep Throat's mind, Barnett said that ideally I needed to make sure I had the person's permission. That permission must be given voluntarily, absolutely and under circumstances that established it was given competently, he said. Voluntarily, absolutely and competently—high standards but the right standards, he said. He suggested that he rough out a proposed sworn affidavit for this person to sign. It was to be an ironclad document, signed by four people—Deep Throat, a competent family member, Deep Throat's lawyer and his doctor. The three witnesses would establish that the permission was given voluntarily and competently.

It was the perfect Barnett document—all thought through to make sure there would be no doubt. But the world of confidential sources always seems to include some doubt. Washington politics and secrets are an entire world of doubt.

I took his draft and attempted to rework it. I had never had a signed agreement with any source before, during or after I received information. Why start now? Would it set a precedent? Paper agreements exist when there is an absence of trust. Well, that pretty much defined the situation. But Barnett's standard—voluntarily, absolutely and competently—was impossible in this case. The "competently" was unattainable for sure. And what would "voluntarily" and "absolutely" mean in these circumstances? I abandoned the idea of a signed affidavit.

AROUND THIS TIME, John Dean had been saying publicly that he was going to publish a 30,000-word e-book identifying Deep Throat on the 30th anniversary of the Watergate burglary, June 17, 2002. He called me, and I said I was no longer going to comment on the subject—period. I would not even rule out absurd suggestions. Many people had died, I had eliminated several publicly. The list was getting shorter, too short.

Mike Wallace of CBS television, a longtime Deep Throat hunter, called seeking a comment because 60 *Minutes* was thinking of doing a segment on Dean's book. I told Wallace I didn't even want to hear the name that Dean had come up with. Wallace mentioned a name. It was wrong and out of the question.

"No comment, period," I said.

"We're not going to do the story," Wallace said. The person had convincingly denied it and had threatened a lawsuit. Dean's e-book publisher was now nervous, Wallace added. Dean's book, *Unmasking Deep Throat,* came out later with no unmasking—only a list of possibles.

Dean opened his 150-page e-book with a quote from Sir Arthur Conan Doyle, creator of Sherlock Holmes, that after excluding the impossible, "whatever remains, however improbable, must be the truth." He closed with another Conan Doyle quote about the importance and prominence of data. "It is a capital mistake to theorize before one has data. Insensibly, one begins to twist facts to suit theories, instead of theories to suit facts." Dean concludes his book, "With that thought in mind, I've little doubt the first person to complete sorting the facts will have everyone saying—why didn't I think of that?"

Dean made the sort of mistake that Arthur Conan Doyle warned of. He theorized that because Deep Throat knew the Nixon White House, he must have actually worked within the Nixon White House. After all, Dean's own formative experience was at the Nixon White House. He never could get around that. Like many people who worked in the White Houses of numerous administrations, Dean could not appreciate that an outsider could see, know and piece together its true nature. Those who are in the orbit, but nonetheless on the edges, can often be the real discoverers. It is why at times, the journalist, the historian and even the novelist paints the fullest picture of an era.

ON JUNE 11, 2002, I reached Joan Felt by phone.

How is he? I asked. She had mentioned the other night that he was frail.

"Yeah, maybe not that frail," Joan said, explaining that he went in and out. "The lawyer was over telling Dad that Deep Throat would be looked at as a hero today and certainly I see it that way. I'm still kind of stunned that my dad had the originality and the kind of independence."

Posing Bradlee's question, saying it was the one I had to ask: Do I owe allegiance to a man who because of age or something else is in a way no longer that man?

Ummmmhhhhhh, Joan said. I sensed that she understood.

In other words, I asked, What are someone's real wishes?

I realized I still had to hedge with her about whether her father had been Deep Throat. If I acknowledged it directly, nothing could prevent her from going out and saying, "Woodward told me my dad was Deep Throat." At the same time I wanted to be honest with her. How? I was fumbling but I finally said that I was not going to answer whether he was Deep Throat or not. But, I said, it was obvious that at some point he helped me.

"You're not going to tell me," she said.

I said that he had been a kind of Lone Ranger on something important. And I would not identify any source until after his death. I wasn't going to change the rules. I would need permission. It needs to be given voluntarily, it needs to be absolute and it needs to be competently given—in other words I have to know this is the same person I was dealing with years ago, I said.

Joan reminded me that it was not my recent visit to Santa Rosa that set the Deep Throat question in motion. "It was really Yvette, Dad's friend, who told me that he was Deep Throat. Whether right or wrong. At least she told me that he had told her he was." She calculated that that had been about 20 years ago.

You realize we know each other, I said.

"You and Dad?"

"Yes."

"Yeah," she agreed.

Not just in passing, not best friends but we know each other, I said.

"And he remembers you, which is unusual," she said. "And that's quite unusual, Bob."

My worry, I said, was that if he said something publicly about our relationship, then he might say the opposite the next time. Or he might say he did not remember. The embedded denials of a former FBI man might be triggered. I didn't want to do anything that might open him to any criticism or ridicule. I said that it was smart of Nancy Reagan to keep former President Reagan out of the spotlight so that people would remember the guy on horseback. There was an image of Reagan as president telling Gorbachev to tear down that wall—a guy in control, strong—that was the image that would last.

Joan said her dad was not strong. "Seeing him shuffle to the bathroom, and it's so hard for him to walk, he's just barely making it. Dad would have said when he was 40 or so, pathetic." Yet she added, "He has this new thing that I don't remember when I was a girl. He has this sweetness that kind of oozes off his face."

I said it would be his words that would be remembered.

"If we decided to disclose whatever the truth is," she said, "we could certainly control all that. We can do like Nancy Reagan. We don't have to allow other people to come in and interview him."

I realized she had no idea what it would be like to have 50 camera crews on their front lawn clamoring for a sighting or a word. He would have to be credible, I said. In other words, his memory has to be real and credible and original. As best I can tell, he does not have a credible memory on a whole range of subjects.

"No he doesn't," Joan said. "You're right." She said that I could revisit my agreement with him and say, "Shall we disclose this before you die or shall we after?"

I cringed. I did not want to discuss his death with him. I then reminded her that she had told me that he had been distressed the other night when this all came up and had been up that night.

"But he quickly got over that. But you're right, we want to protect him." Then she said, "It would be great to disclose. And I'm able to say, 'Dad, you did that! That was so cool.'"

I said I had to protect myself and I had to protect my sources. That would require being convinced that there is voluntary, absolute and competently given permission. And that time might have passed.

"Yes," she said.

JOAN SAID SHE WOULD CALL ME back when she found some notes of her conversations with her dad. She called back several minutes later.

John O'Connor, Mark Felt's grandson Nick, and Joan had talked with Felt on Sunday. "John was just presenting a case that Deep Throat was a good guy and that people would think highly of him."

Later, she said, her dad had taken a long drive with his caregiver, and her dad had said, "It might threaten the security of my family. 'What would my parents think?' An-

other question was, 'What would they think in the Bureau?'
He was worried about that. He kept talking about it, just
kept talking about it, which is unlike him because he usually doesn't stay with one subject or conversation for a long
period on his own."

She also reported that he said, "I'd only talk if you could
prove that Deep Throat is a national hero. Otherwise I'm
going to deny it."

After she had read her notes I asked if she thought her
dad had been Deep Throat.

She went back and forth, just like her dad.

I said that she should not try to read me. Based on what
your dad has said recently, what's your conclusion?

"My conclusion is yes, that he is. I think it is wonderful.
Yeah, I guess that's true. And also a surprise. A big surprise. Kind of an exciting incident in our family. That's why
I would like to be able to share it with Dad while he's still
alive, just talk about it, help him remember so that he can
appreciate whatever part he played in history. Obviously, he
played some part in history."

I said that two years ago when I talked to him, I had concluded that he did not have sufficient credible memory to
vouch for anything going back to his FBI days.

"Well, I'm sure it hasn't gotten any better," she said.

Exactly, I said. I spent hours with him and I went through
a lot of things.

"On that visit?" she asked.

Yes.

"Doesn't remember," she said. "It's interesting that he re-members you. I cannot think of anybody from that era of his life that he does."

He has reason to remember me, I said, but I cannot falsely unlock his memory.

"The fact that he has some kind of bond with you is quite extraordinary," she said. "He doesn't remember Ed Miller and the other FBI guys. He remembers J. Edgar Hoover."

Well, I thought, Hoover and me.

16

———

HOW MIGHT MORE BE UNLOCKED? I WONDERED. What was accessible that might be genuine and true? I was haunted by the divide between who Mark had been as a source and the man who made repeated, bald denials, his public insistence for so long that he had not been Deep Throat, even though he had now acknowledged it. The denials only solidified my sad understanding that anyone in a jam—or believes he is in a jam—will say anything to protect and extricate himself.

Over time, we all become committed to a version of the story of our lives. Simplification and repetition solidify the account, and we tend to stick with that identity. But that is old news. Yet precisely what was the dilemma he faced after he was pardoned by Reagan?

I am disappointed and a little angry at both myself and him for never digging out a more exacting explanation, a clearer statement of his reasoning and motivation.

Peter Gay, one of Sigmund Freud's biographers, attempted to reduce Freud's insights to a single idea and came pretty close. Gay wrote that personality is really not the resolution of an individual's various impulses but rather the organization of those impulses. In other words, one's less desirable impulses, desires or inclinations are often not conquered, but fit into a life hopefully dominated by the more desirable impulses. So contradictions abound. Any attempt I might make to explain or resolve or fully make sense of Mark Felt's behavior would probably fail.

At the same time, there is a certain consistency—even a nobility and surely courage—in what Felt did if you adopt J. Edgar Hoover's overall view of the FBI's role in the United States government. I find it frightening, but in this view the Bureau is a pillar that stands to protect law-abiding citizens, and if in that process the FBI had to become a law unto itself, so be it. The bank robbers, gangsters, mobsters, domestic terrorists, foreign spies, philandering civil rights leaders, corrupt politicians and even presidents were all formidable foes. But the FBI could eventually beat them all.

It was the Nixon administration that presented the most serious challenge to the Bureau, because it was an attempted takeover from the top. The installation of Pat Gray as director threatened the institution. So the FBI was at war, though not with the usual suspects. The war was with Nixon and his men. So Felt took to the underground parking garage. He never really voiced pure, raw outrage to me about Watergate or what it represented. The crimes and abuses were background music. Nixon was trying to subvert not only the law but the Bureau. So Watergate became Felt's instrument to reassert the Bureau's independence and thus its supremacy. In the end, the Bureau was damaged, seriously but not permanently, while Nixon lost much more, maybe everything—the presidency, power, and whatever moral authority he might have had. He was disgraced.

By surviving and enduring his hidden life, in contrast and in his own way, Mark Felt won.

IT WAS LEONARD GARMENT who provided another perspective on the story in October 2000. Frank Wills, the security guard at the Watergate, was paid $80 a week. His discovery of a door taped twice and his call to the police triggered a series of accidents that led to Nixon's resignation. Wills had lived a disappointing life and had some years earlier complained bitterly that he had not received the rewards he deserved. He died of a brain tumor at 52.

Garment went on to say that "the largest accident of Watergate" was Deep Throat, who provided the organizing idea behind our coverage in the *Post*. The contrast between

Frank Wills and Deep Throat could not have been greater, Garment said.

"Frank Wills, having by accident become famous and historic, was cast aside in the usual way when history and fame grew bored with him. Deep Throat was much too sophisticated to let that happen to him."

It was an interesting notion, but I don't think it was sophistication. It was fear. By insisting that his identity be preserved, Garment speculated, Deep Throat was able to live as he chose, entirely out of the spotlight, unencumbered by scrutiny or analysis of his motives—free. Garment thought that Deep Throat had wisely dodged the bullet of fame, and suggested his quality of life was his just and appropriate reward.

I kept in touch with Joan periodically. By the summer of 2004 we were exchanging e-mails. I mentioned that I had visited my own father, a retired state judge, who was now approaching 91 and living in a nursing home in Illinois. My father did not remember much, I said, but he seemed content.

On August 4, 2004, Joan e-mailed. "Yes, Dad is happy too. And SO LOVING!!!"

Before Christmas I received a holiday greeting letter which Joan had composed from Mark to a group of friends. It was signed with a shaky, feeble but legible "Mark," no longer the dramatic and authoritative "F" of his Bureau days. Included was a picture of her father standing out-doors in the sun with his caretaker, Bola. Felt had the smile of the ages on his face—the man who, as much as anyone, had confounded and beat Richard Nixon.

AGAIN AND AGAIN I retraced my steps, the notes, the books, testimony, an occasional lunch with an old Watergate player and, most important, I sifted decades of memory. Mark was now shielded from my effort at interrogation, and even his own self-interrogation. There were many questions that we would never get to. Highly trained and focused, Mark was a product of that FBI pyramid—the hierarchy and the Hoover rules. The climax for Mark Felt was the year 1972—Vietnam, the perceived domestic threat, law and order challenged, the presidential election and all its in-tensity, the Wallace shooting, the death of Hoover, the unexpected directorship of Pat Gray, Watergate, thwarted ambition, and the insistence of a young reporter.

Watergate moved history, and there is certainly a tendency—on my part and of many others—to associate epic outcome with an epic motive. Perhaps that is an un-necessary stretch. Felt's motives certainly were complicated and not fully explainable. But three decades in the FBI had steeped him in one basic principle: The truth will come out. And in that, in Watergate and in Nixon's demise, there was a sense of rough justice. And that, maybe, is enough.

. . .

I WAS HOPING to put down the full story, as I have attempted to do here. I wanted it to be clear, straightforward, nothing held back. The portrait of me is not all that admirable. I was pushy, secretive, I used Mark Felt, and I lied to a colleague, Richard Cohen. But I wanted this account to be the antidote to Watergate, which had always been so convoluted, things always being concealed. Because that strange and compelling era played such an important part in my life, I kept going back to it.

There is probably no period in history about which we know so much, no presidency that has been on the autopsy table to have every part dissected and rummaged through so entirely. The multiple investigations, the endless memoirs and diaries, the memos and notes—no one keeps anything close to an equivalent record now. The testimony and trials and the thousands of hours of secret tape recordings—Nixon talking to everyone, everyone talking to him, Nixon on the phone, Nixon going on and on. Virtually everyone in Nixon's inner circle finally turned on him— testified or wrote a book, telling about his bitterness and anger and his efforts to break the law and to use his presidential power to settle new and old scores with his enemies, real and imagined. There is so much that no one will ever be able to digest it all. But this autopsy seems nearly complete.

But then, of course, there are always unanswered questions. Those questions lead to more questions, with the circularity of the endless inquest, keeping people like me in business. We can and should always poke at the questions of motivation. And we will. There never is a final draft of history.

A Reporter's Assessment

By Carl Bernstein

THE DAY AFTER MEMORIAL DAY, TUESDAY, MAY 31, 2005, *Vanity Fair* magazine sent me an article to be released that morning. It was headlined "I'm the Guy They Called Deep Throat," written by the Felt family lawyer, John O'Connor. He and Joan Felt had persuaded her father to let them assert that he had been our secret source. O'Connor acknowledged in the article that Felt's memory was all but erased.

I am a contributing editor to *Vanity Fair*, but I had no clue this was coming. I called Bob, who had received his copy of the article in Washington.

We had lived with this secret for 33 years—and were accustomed to the occasional book or the latest theory or university study that claimed to have established Deep Throat's identity. Each time one of the Deep Throat suspects—and there were dozens—died, we fielded media calls from reporters asking if this was the one. The list had narrowed as the men of Watergate passed away. We adopted a rigid stance—no more comment until Deep Throat had died.

It was essential that we not break faith with Felt, nor violate the journalistic principle of protecting the confidentiality of a source. *Vanity Fair* offered no new evidence that Felt was Deep Throat other than a single quotation attributed to him—"I'm the guy they used to call Deep Throat." Without our confirmation, it seemed the secret might still hold. With Bob's agreement, I issued a statement to CNN: "As we have said consistently, when the individual known as Deep Throat dies, we will disclose his identity and the circumstances and context of our dealings with him. Numerous speculative books and articles have been written about his identity, and in this latest instance, we again note that we have an obligation to all our confidential sources, not to abrogate our pledge to them that we will not reveal their identities during their lifetimes. So when this individual—Deep Throat—dies, we will then disclose his identity, as we have always promised."

"Just right," Bob said, "but a little long." A few minutes later one of the television networks cut away from live coverage of President Bush's press conference to report on *Vanity Fair's* article and my statement.

Bob told me that Ben Bradlee, who had retired as editor 14 years earlier and was now the *Post's* vice president at large, was eager to confirm it. "They've got it!" He still recognized a scoop when he saw one. The lawyer and the family were sufficient, more than sufficient, to release the *Post* from our agreement, he had said.

I KNEW THAT BOB, who is prone to complete his homework before it is due or even assigned, had written a book-length draft of the Deep Throat story.

In March Bob had agreed to have Bradlee's successor, Leonard Downie Jr., come to his house to read the draft, and for the first time learn the identity of Deep Throat. Downie assured Bob he would tell no one, but he was insistent *The Washington Post* be prepared to cover Deep Throat's death. Bob, as an assistant managing editor, reports to Downie.

In early 2005, there had been news articles saying that Deep Throat might be near death. Downie wanted a plan. Another reporter would write the story of Deep Throat's death and Bob could write about his relationship with Felt.

Now that the *Vanity Fair* article was out, Bob filled me in on this background. I was worried that we were losing control of the story. We had forgotten one of journalism's basic tenets: Reporters may believe they control the story, but the story always controls the reporters.

I spent the rest of the morning answering calls from the media, and I wanted to get to Washington and the *Post*, where the decisions were being made. On my way to the airport, I phoned Bob. By then he had talked to Downie, who was at a corporate retreat in St. Michael's, Maryland, two hours away on the other side of the Chesapeake Bay. Downie had ordered a full package of stories but maintained he could pull back.

About 2:30 P.M. Bob went to the *Post* on 15th Street Northwest in downtown Washington. Len had just arrived. The two of them went into Downie's office and closed the door. This was the same office where Bradlee, Bob and I along with the other *Post* editors debated the decisions on the Watergate stories more than three decades earlier, though now the office furniture and decor had been upgraded.

"I'm more and more convinced—this is truly it," Len said. He had now read the article. O'Connor and Joan Felt surely had credibility. Bob had been dealing with them for several years on this. They had not parachuted in. They were Felt's caregiver-daughter and the family lawyer. What more could we want? "Clearly, clearly" this freed all of us from the confidentiality commitment, Downie said. "This is hard for you, I know," he added. "This is hard to give up." He knew that secrets have a power, and as long as Bob and I controlled the secret, we had the power.

Bob held fast. Five years earlier, when he had met with Felt in California, the former No. 2 man at the FBI couldn't remember the circumstances of Nixon's resignation. Should we be letting these family surrogates and *Vanity Fair* make our decision? Bob asked Downie.

"They already have," Len said. "Bob, it's over."

Was Downie sure that confirmation would be sound journalistically and institutionally for the *Post*?

Yes. There would never be a better moment, Downie said. He suggested that this was an opportunity. If we were to wait until Felt's death to make the disclosure, there would be doubt. The *Post's* critics and others in the press might say in effect, "How convenient." Felt would be unable to deny or confirm his role. The controversy would never end.

Downie was suggesting that the *Vanity Fair* disclosure, backed by our confirmation, might bring an unusual clarity and even "closure" to the issue. He had consulted with Bradlee and Don Graham, the CEO of the *Post*. They agreed with him.

I recognized that this was an example of the boss, having already made a decision, taking the time to bring along the subordinate. He didn't want just our acquiescence, he wanted our full agreement. At the same time, no doubt, he wanted to see if there were any arguments that had not yet been advanced. Downie had been an investigative reporter in the 1960s before he became an editor. He knows the importance of confidential sources as well as Bob and I do.

Okay, Bob finally said. First, he would have to discuss this with me and make sure I agreed. He then would go along.

Bob went down the hall to his office and called me. I said the decision might already be out of our hands. We could not be the only ones to refuse comment or confirmation of the obvious. Bob wondered if the train had left the station. "It probably has," I told him. "We can't be the assholes." But I wanted the confirmation to come from us, not the *Post*, and Bob agreed.

THE SUMMER OF 1972 was the first time I'd heard about Bob's secret source. This was before the managing editor, Howard Simons, dubbed him Deep Throat. Bob said he was in the Justice Department, in a good position, an old friend from his Navy days.

Sounded good to me. Over the years I had gotten to know a few people in the Justice building on Pennsylvania Avenue, which then also housed the FBI. I had some sources in various divisions, a judge picker or two and some G-men, who were useful when I covered the local and federal courts.

As Bob and I progressed in our coverage of the Watergate story it became apparent that his source—"my friend," as he called him—had command of an extraordinary body of information. The problem was that he wouldn't part with it easily, or too willingly. When I pressed Bob to tell me more about his friend, he was uncharacteristically skittish. He wouldn't tell me his name at first, only that he was in the FBI and had an office just outside Acting Director Pat Gray's. Every piece of information, report, file or telegram, Bob said, that crossed Gray's desk, crossed his friend's.

For several months I formed a picture of Bob's friend as a young man who was something of a gatekeeper to Gray. I pictured a small glass-enclosed cubicle outside the paneled quarters of the boss. Because of the Navy connection, my assumption was that Bob and his friend were contemporaries. Hence my mental picture of a lean, clean-cut, close-cropped FBI type, fresh up from the FBI Academy at Quantico, Virginia, shuffling and arranging the paperwork and the files that flowed into Gray's office. A gofer. But a gofer with a hell of a view.

In the fall of 1972 when we published some of our most important stories and the White House escalated its public attacks on us and the *Post*, I told Bob I needed to know the name of his source. Bob said it was Mark Felt. The name was less important to me than the fact that he was the No. 2 man in the Bureau. I was impressed. It meant that our source could provide all-important context. But we were busy and scrambling for more information. The pressure was immense, and there was no time to discuss the broader ramifications.

As recounted in *All the President's Men,* during this period Bob and I would often meet for coffee in a little vending machine room off the newsroom floor. These were our strategy sessions. Just the two of us, and really bad cups of coffee. We reviewed the status of where we were on each story, and discussed what kind of presentation we would make that day to our editors. Sometimes, we thought, they were awfully slow to recognize the value of a particular piece of our work. We had elaborate good-cop/bad-cop routines that we more or less rehearsed over the coffee. Usually I was the bad cop.

One of our conversations in the vending machine room was intentionally left out of *All the President's Men.*

During that fall of 1972, we had established that there was a secret cash slush fund maintained by the Nixon re-election committee CREEP. It had financed the Watergate break-in operation and other campaign espionage and sabotage. The key to discovering the possible involvement by higher-ups was this fund. The CREEP treasurer, Hugh Sloan, and the bookkeeper, Judy Hoback, had after several days of teeth-pulling interview sessions told us that John Mitchell was one of the five who controlled the fund. Deep

Throat had confirmed this. Mitchell, Nixon's former law partner, former campaign manager and former attorney general of the United States, was the ultimate higher-up. The man. And we were about to write a story saying that the man was a criminal.

As we were reviewing the story and its implications, I put a coin into the coffee machine and experienced a literal chill going down my neck—a sensation sufficiently vivid, unanticipated and unprecedented that I recall it even now with almost a shudder.

"Oh my God," I said to Bob. My back was to him. I turned. "This president is going to be impeached."

Bob sat motionless. He looked at me for a second or two in the strangest way. But it was not a look of skepticism or any sense of dismissing what I had said—not the look he delivered at times on my occasional flights of fancy.

"Jesus, I think you're right," said the staid man from the Midwest.

It had not occurred to me that such a thought had crossed his mind too. Even the most partisan Nixon-haters to our knowledge had not suggested such a possibility. It was only three months after the break-in at the Watergate. It would be another 12 months before Congress took up impeachment, and 22 months before Nixon resigned. "We can never use that word in this newsroom," Bob said.

I saw the point. Our editors might think we had an

agenda or that our reporting was overreaching or even that we had gone around the bend. Any suggestion about the future of the Nixon presidency could undermine our work and the *Post*'s effort to be fair.

We did not tell this story in *All the President's Men* because the book was published in April 1974 in the midst of the House Judiciary Committee's impeachment investigation of President Nixon. To recount it then might have given the impression that impeachment had been our goal all along. It was not. It was always about the story.

Over the years, Bob and I have talked about that vending machine moment many times. We had both reached this same conclusion about the possibility of impeachment because we had an array of sources at all levels—secretaries, the campaign treasurer, the bookkeeper, lawyers, former Nixon aides and friends, and Deep Throat. People will and should debate the significance and role of any of the sources. But the essential point is rather simple. It was the convergence of all the sources, not just a single one, but these firsthand witnesses at all levels, that enabled us to penetrate the secrecy of the Nixon presidency.

I ARRIVED AT THE SHUTTLE terminal at Reagan National Airport and took a cab to the *Post*. The newsroom was eerily quiet, and it took me a moment to realize why. During my years at the *Post*, the clatter of typewriters was incessant as deadlines approached. Now there was only the subdued clicking of computer keyboards. Downie greeted me with a hug, then Bradlee with another hug. Bob and I embraced and held each other briefly. There was a whole lifetime of emotions and journalism in this moment.

So Bob, 62, and I, 61, walked a few paces out into the newsroom, that austere, brightly lit arena of so many years of our lives. It had been vividly and accurately portrayed in the movie version of *All the President's Men*. I felt regret—I'm not sure about what—but also an immense sense of relief.

We had said publicly over the last several decades that for a reporter, all good work was done in defiance of management. That meant the reporter had to set his or her own course, had to push back against editors at times, to roam and be free to explore, to defy the conventional wisdom if necessary. It meant that reporters, whatever they covered, had to find the inside stories, get to the bottom of things, and find the Bookkeepers and the Deep Throats if possible. At the same time, as we had just been reminded, reporters need editors. In the end we are collaborators and they make the final calls.

After all, that was what the Watergate reporting had been about—partnerships. My partnership with Bob, and ours with Bradlee, and Bob's strange and incomplete partnership with Deep Throat. In all, it added up to a feeling of solidarity. Today's Internet bloggers and television's talking heads don't have that. No safety net. No brakes. No one there to question, doubt or inspire. No editor.

Out in the glare of the newsroom we found the reporter who was writing the main story for the *Post*.

This was our statement: "W. Mark Felt was Deep Throat and helped us immeasurably in our Watergate coverage. However, as the record shows, many other sources and officials assisted us and other reporters for the hundreds of stories written in *The Washington Post*."

Author's Note

TWO COLLEAGUES HELPED ME NIGHT AND DAY during the crash, 10-day period in which this book was made ready for publication from a confidential manuscript I had written in case Mark Felt died:

Bill Murphy Jr., an attorney who has practiced at the U.S. Department of Justice and in the Army Judge Advocate General's Corps. A former reporter for the *New Haven Register*, Bill is a man of immense brainpower and grace. He provided an independent, critical evaluation of each part of this story through the wise eye of lawyer and journalist. He joined me only five weeks before the identity of Deep Throat was revealed. I already consider him my trusted partner.

Christine Parthemore, a 2003 Phi Beta Kappa political science graduate of The Ohio State University. Resourceful, mature and dogged, Christine is able to find anything or anyone. A woman of disarming frankness and amazing creativity, she has assisted me with great skill and precision on a wide variety of projects since we began working together in May 2004. She is a full member of our reporting and writing team.

Acknowledgments

THE SECRET MAN IS THE PRODUCT OF MORE THAN three decades of reporting. Simon & Schuster and *The Washington Post* have been stalwarts throughout my career, and their support was crucial once again as I wrote this book. They have given me the time, independence and ability to pursue these stories.

Watergate forever fused Carl Bernstein's name with mine. I will always be grateful for the partnership we forged, and for his friendship.

Alice Mayhew has been my trusted editor at Simon & Schuster on every book I've written. The day after Carl and I acknowledged that Mark Felt was Deep Throat, Alice flew to Washington to read my draft of this story for the first time. She demonstrated her tireless dedication to her authors once more, contributing countless ideas and improvements.

Ben Bradlee, the executive editor of *The Washington Post* through Watergate and other tumultuous times, kept his faith in Carl and me and our reporting, and kept the Deep Throat secret for more than 30 years. He read an early draft of this story and made invaluable suggestions. He is my confidant and true friend.

Leonard Downie Jr. succeeded Bradlee as the *Post's* executive editor in 1991, and he played an important role in the final chapter of this tale. I am also very much indebted to Don Graham, the *Post's* chief executive officer, and Bo Jones, the publisher. They are all first-rate, major reasons why the *Post* has achieved and maintained its reputation for excellent journalism.

Bill Hamilton, the *Post's* assistant managing editor for enterprise, did the impossible in about 24 hours: He took the entire first draft of this story and found a way to do a short adaptation that ran in *The Washington Post* two days after Deep Throat's identity was announced. His effort was impressive, but no surprise to me.

Joe Elbert, the photo editor at the *Post*, and Melissa Maltby in the photo department provided files of old and new photos in less than a day, and for this I thank them.

Stan Pottinger, who discovered Deep Throat's identity in 1976, showed incredible restraint in keeping Deep Throat's identity a secret for 29 years. I am grateful for his admirable discretion.

Robert Barnett has been my lawyer and good friend for two decades. His advice on this book—both as a lawyer and early reader—was invariably correct. I am grateful for his counsel, and for that of Tom Hentoff, one of his partners at the law firm Williams & Connolly.

At Simon & Schuster, Carolyn Reidy, the president, and David Rosenthal, the publisher, made sure the process of rushing this book to the presses was rapid and efficient. I am also indebted to Jack Romanos, the president and chief executive officer; Elisa Rivlin, the general counsel; Victoria Meyer, the executive director of publicity; Jackie Seow, the art director; Roger Labrie, editor; Irene Kheradi, the executive managing editor; Karen Romano, vice president, production and manufacturing; Twisne Fan, director of production; C. Linda Dingler, director of design; Jane Hardick, desktop publishing manager; Barbara Greenberg, Carla Little, Claudia Martinez, and Davina Mock, desktop publishing staff; Nancy Inglis, director of copyediting; Mara Lurie, Lisa Healy, and Jane Elias, proofreaders; Chris Carruth, indexer; as well as Allison Murray, Annie Railton and Kenneth Hamner.

Fred Chase, who copyedited both *Bush at War* and *Plan of Attack*, flew from Texas to Washington, D.C., on short notice to copyedit this manuscript. He did an excellent job, and the final version is better for his countless contributions.

My two daughters, Diana and Tali, keep me grounded and add the greatest joy and humor to my life. I am proud of them and can never thank them enough for their love and support.

My wife, Elsa, has guided and counseled me for 25 years on virtually every issue in my life, not least of which were the questions of when and how to properly disclose Deep Throat's identity. Her wisdom, patience and support sustain me.

Thanks again to Rosa Criollo and Jackie Crowe. Eternal love and thanks to the late Norma Gianelloni.

I will always be grateful to the many sources who spoke with us as we reported on Watergate, and who have spoken with me and my colleagues on countless stories and books over the years. The free press cannot fulfill its vital, constitutional role without these people.

Finally, I will forever be grateful to W. Mark Felt. It was a tug-of-war at times, but he came through, providing the kind of guidance, information and understanding that were essential to the Watergate story.

Index